Those They Left Behind ...

Those They Left Behind ...

World War II Photographs of German Soldiers with their Wives, Families, and Sweethearts

Kriegsmarine • Heer • Luftwaffe
NSDAP • SS • Polizei • SA • HJ

Frank Holford and Branislav Radovic

Schiffer Military History
Atglen, PA

Acknowledgements
The authors would like to thank: Andy Bellinger (editor extraordinaire) for his much appreciated help and patience, Colin Kluth, Michael Burroughs, Malcolm & Daniel Fisher at Regimentals.com and Bob Tredwen at MilitaryAntiques.com who generously donated material and Richard Holford who helped with the technical stuff.

Book design by Branislav Radovic and Robert Biondi.

Library of Congress Catalog Number: 2010940667

Printed in Hong Kong.
ISBN: 978-0-7643-3768-0

We are always looking for people to write books on new and related subjects. If you have an idea for a book, please contact us at the address below.

Published by Schiffer Publishing Ltd.
4880 Lower Valley Road
Atglen, PA 19310
Phone: (610) 593-1777
FAX: (610) 593-2002
E-mail: Info@schifferbooks.com.
Visit our web site at: www.schifferbooks.com
Please write for a free catalog.
This book may be purchased from the publisher.
Please include $5.00 postage.
Try your bookstore first.

In Europe, Schiffer books are distributed by:
Bushwood Books
6 Marksbury Ave.
Kew Gardens, Surrey TW9 4JF
England
Phone: 44 (0)20 8392-8585
FAX: 44 (0)20 8392-9876
E-mail: info@bushwoodbooks.co.uk
www.bushwoodbooks.co.uk

FOREWORD

This book records, in pictures, the weddings of Germans during the Third Reich period. Some are groups of family and friends. Some are weddings by proxy where the marriage ceremony is conducted near the front with a picture of the bride and also on the home front with a picture of the groom. Sometimes a steel helmet was used in place of a photograph in the home front weddings. To marry, a number of requirements had to be met. For example racial purity had to be proved by examination of the family tree, permission had to be given to marry a foreigner (auslander). In effect the state had to be satisfied and a law was passed in Nuremberg to achieve this.

Ranks and service qualifications are shown, as well as changes in the uniforms as the war continued, possibly due to needs and shortages. Some of the men are wearing the dress daggers which were used on formal occasions and some grooms are seen wearing a sprig on the left breast of the uniform which may indicate that they are of the Christian faith. Variations in the brides' dresses can be of interest to female readers showing the styles of the period. In one photograph Hitler's personal guard is seen as a wedding guest. Also included are wedding thank you letters, pages from the NSDAP Wedding Service Guide, an SS Application to Marry document and charts illustrating the "Party View" on marriage and procuration.

Frank Holford

PREFACE

Studio portraits, particularly wedding photographs, taken under near-perfect conditions, can be a great source of reference for the uniform collector and offer an alternative to the more familiar images that appear in reference books.

These posed and (for the student of warfare) pedestrian photographs, far from the horrors of the front, are often neglected as a reference source in military history books that wish to capture the essence of combat and the fighting man at war.

However, at the very heart of what sustained the fighting man were thoughts of home and loved ones. Whether in the boredom of garrison life or the desperate and violent world of combat, it is the memories of those he left behind that provided a tenuous link to normality and hope for the future. It was the wedding photograph that provided a tangible reminder of happier times and the promise of a new life.

When we look at the photographs of these men and their loved ones we can see real people with hopes, fears and joys, not just the uniforms, weapons and equipment, so often the focus of other reference works. The photographs in this book are, in part, about this other side to the combat soldier, highlighting the personal sacrifices that men and women made, and continue to make, during war time.

This book is dedicated to those who, then and now, made that sacrifice.

Branislav Radovic

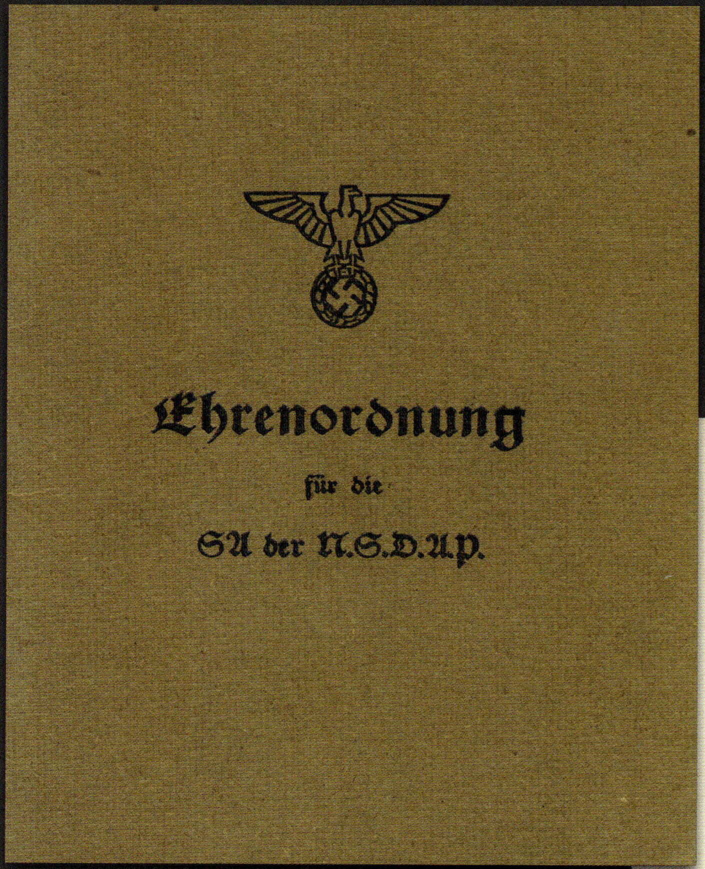

■ The NSDAP Official Order of Marriage, as laid down on the 12th. December 1933.

The front cover, followed by the introduction by Adolf Hitler and lastly a foreword by Sturmabteilung (SA) leader Ernst Röhm.

N.S.D.A.P.
Der Oberste SA-Führer

München, den 12. Dezember 1933.

Ich genehmige die

Ehrenordnung

(E.O.)

für die SA.

Sie gilt für alle der Obersten SA-Führung unterstellten Gliederungen.

Der Oberste SA-Führer:
Adolf Hitler.

Der Oberste SA-Führer.
Chef Nr. 1680/33.

München, den 12. Dezember 1933.

Vorbemerkung.

Mit dem heutigen Tage tritt die nachstehende Ehrenordnung (E.O.) für die SA in Kraft.

Die Anwendung wird zunächst auf die höheren und mittleren Führer der SA beschränkt. Die Ausdehnung auf die gesamte SA wird folgen, wenn die dazu nötigen Erörterungen im Rahmen der Partei abgeschlossen sind.

Wo in der Vorschrift die Bezeichnung SA, SA-Führer oder SA-Männer gebraucht wird, sind damit aktive SA, SS, SAR I, SAR II und NSKK, kurz alle der Obersten SA-Führung unterstellten Gliederungen, sowie deren Angehörige (Führer, Männer und Anwärter) gemeint.

Eigenmächtige Zusätze und Abänderungen sind untersagt.

Der Stabschef:
Röhm.

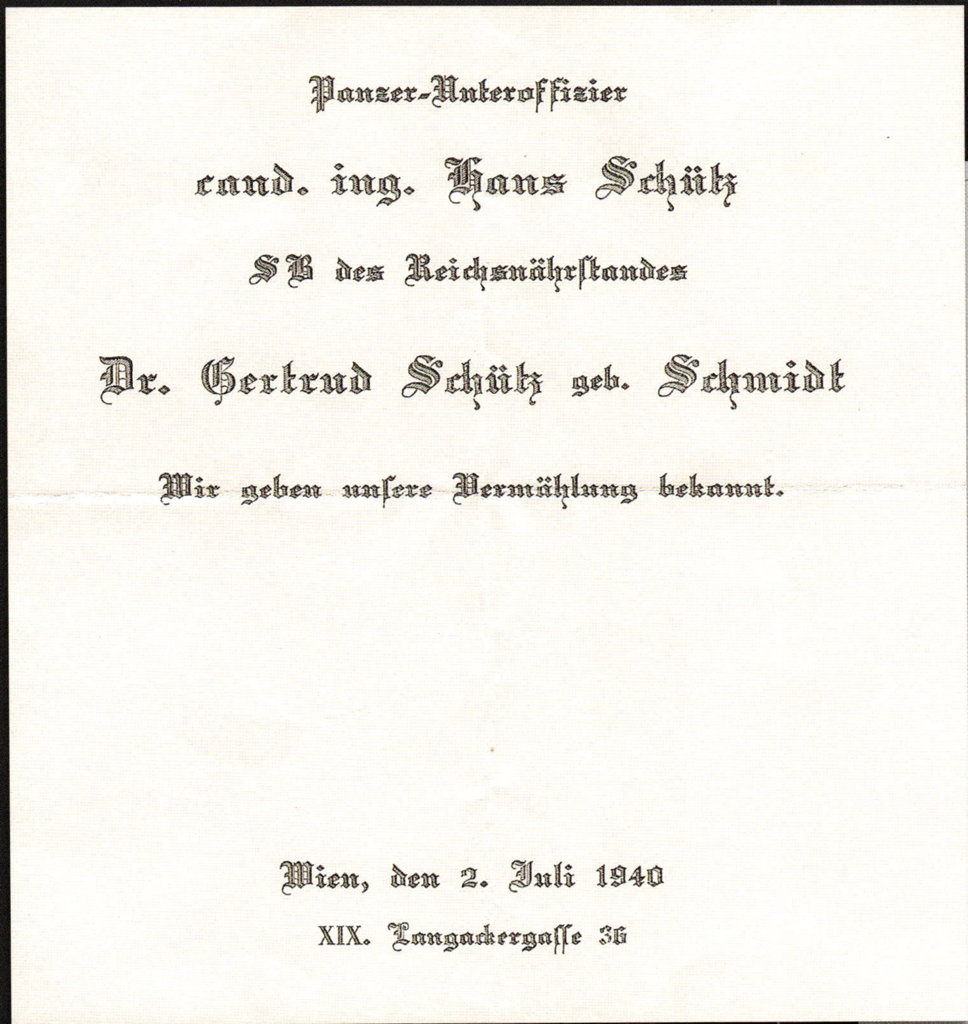

Panzer-Unteroffizier

cand. ing. Hans Schütz

SB des Reichsnährstandes

Dr. Gertrud Schütz geb. Schmidt

Wir geben unsere Vermählung bekannt.

Wien, den 2. Juli 1940

XIX. Langackergasse 36

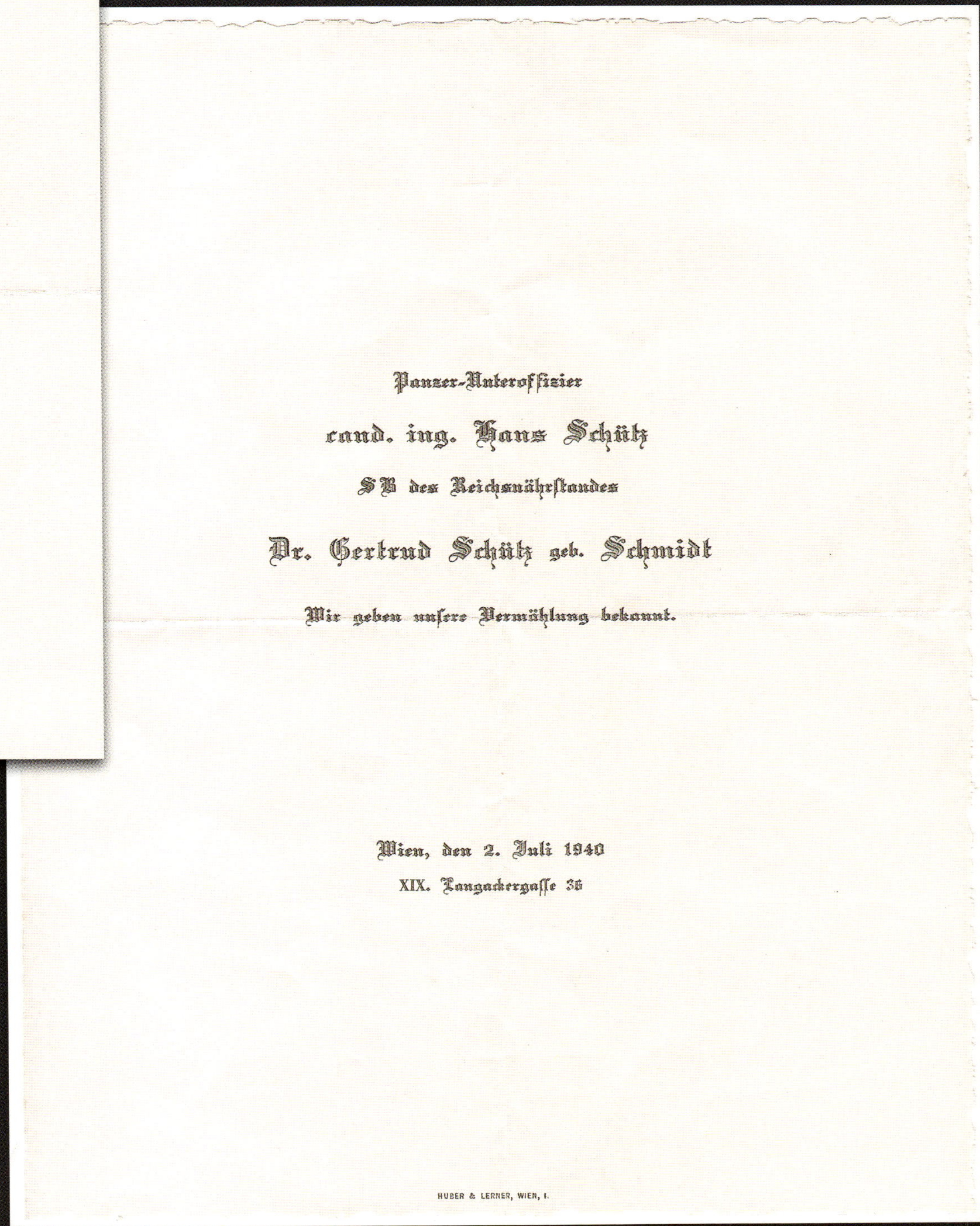

Panzer-Unteroffizier

cand. ing. Hans Schütz

SB des Reichsnährstandes

Dr. Gertrud Schütz geb. Schmidt

Wir geben unsere Vermählung bekannt.

Wien, den 2. Juli 1940

XIX. Langackergasse 36

HUBER & LERNER, WIEN, I.

- This document is a 'thank you' to wedding guests invited to the wedding of:

Panzer Unteroffizier Hans Schutz

Doctor Gertrud Schutz, formerly Schmidt

We give our sincere thanks

Vienna, on the 2nd July 1940

XIX. Langackergasse 36

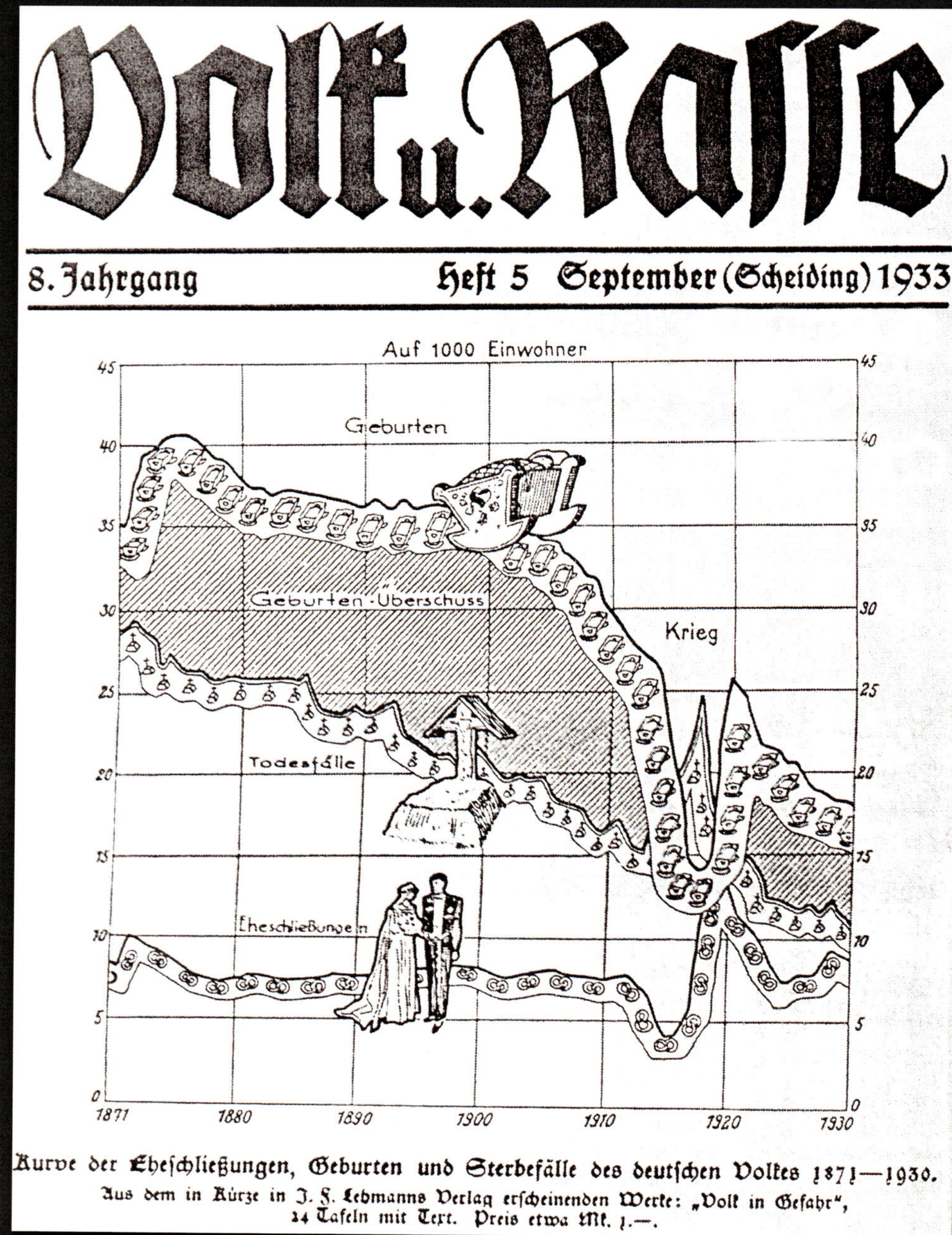

These and the following graphics show the concern the NSDAP had for population growth and general eugenics during the 12 years of the Third Reich.

The title reads: "WE DO NOT STAND ALONE … only genetically healthy offspring enhance the health of the people". This illustration states that since Germany instigated its sterilisation laws in 1933, numerous other countries, shown listed here, have also instituted some form of genetic regulation.

From the publication 'PEOPLE AND RACE'. The chart shows the continued decline in births (per 1,000 inhabitants) after a small increase after the First World War, the general decline in deaths, apart from the obvious rise during the First World War and the virtually unchanged marriage rate.

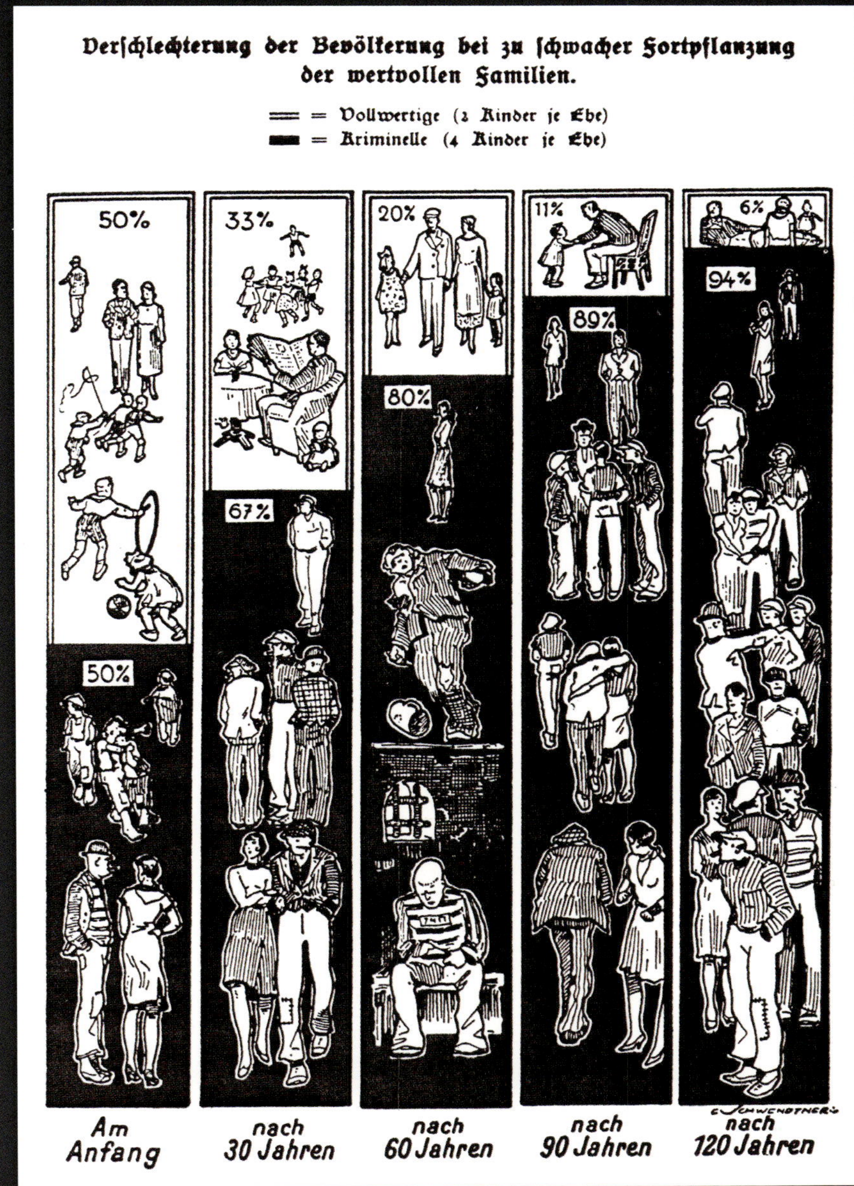

"THE THREAT OF THE SUB-HUMAN
Male Criminals have an average of 4.9 children.
Marriages of the Criminal Classes produce an average of 4.4 children.
Marriages of Slow-learners produce an average of 3.5 children.
The German Family produces an average of 2.2 children.
Marriages of the Educated Classes produce an average of 1.9 children"
(From: Volk in Gefahr, 1937)

"DEGENERATION OF THE POPULATION AS A RESULT OF INSUFFICIENT REPRODUCTION OF VALUABLE FAMILIES"
The chart proports to illustrate the expected growth of criminal families in Germany.
"Today: 50% of the population.
30 years: 67% of the population.
60 years: 80% of the population
80 years: 89% of the population
120 years: 94% of the population"

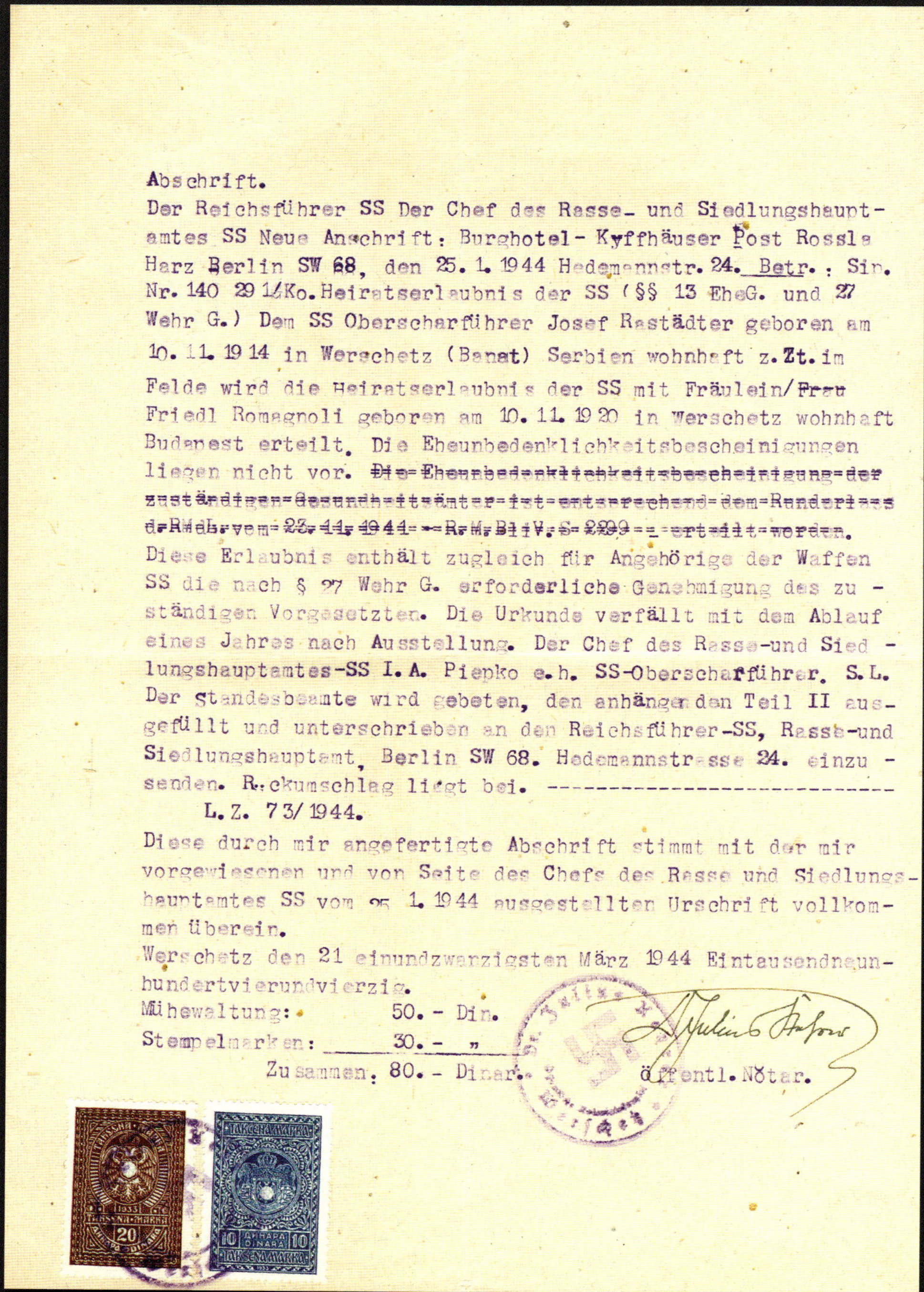

Abschrift.
Der Reichsführer SS Der Chef des Rasse- und Siedlungshauptamtes SS Neue Anschrift: Burghotel- Kyffhäuser Post Rossla Harz Berlin SW 68, den 25. 1. 1944 Hedemannstr. 24. Betr.: Sip. Nr. 140 29 1/Ko. Heiratserlaubnis der SS (§§ 13 EheG. und 27 Wehr G.) Dem SS Oberscharführer Josef Rastädter geboren am 10. 11. 1914 in Werschetz (Banat) Serbien wohnhaft z. Zt. im Felde wird die Heiratserlaubnis der SS mit Fräulein/~~Frau~~ Friedl Romagnoli geboren am 10. 11. 1920 in Werschetz wohnhaft Budapest erteilt. Die Eheunbedenklichkeitsbescheinigungen liegen nicht vor. ~~Die Eheunbedenklichkeitsbescheinigung der zuständigen Gesundheitsämter ist entsprechend dem Runderlass d. RMdI. vom 23. 11. 1944 – R. M. Bl. iV. S. 2299 – erteilt worden.~~
Diese Erlaubnis enthält zugleich für Angehörige der Waffen SS die nach § 27 Wehr G. erforderliche Genehmigung des zuständigen Vorgesetzten. Die Urkunde verfällt mit dem Ablauf eines Jahres nach Ausstellung. Der Chef des Rasse-und Siedlungshauptamtes-SS I. A. Piepko e. h. SS-Oberscharführer. S. L.
Der Standesbeamte wird gebeten, den anhängenden Teil II ausgefüllt und unterschrieben an den Reichsführer-SS, Rasse-und Siedlungshauptamt, Berlin SW 68. Hedemannstrasse 24. einzusenden. Rückumschlag liegt bei. ----------------------------
L. Z. 73/1944.
Diese durch mir angefertigte Abschrift stimmt mit der mir vorgewiesenen und von Seite des Chefs des Rasse und Siedlungshauptamtes SS vom 25. 1. 1944 ausgestellten Urschrift vollkommen überein.
Werschetz den 21 einundzwanzigsten März 1944 Eintausendneunhundertvierundvierzig.
Mühewaltung: 50. - Din.
Stempelmarken: 30. - "
Zusammen: 80. - Dinar. öffentl. Notar.

Copy.
The Reichsführer SS Head of the Race and Settlement Office SS New address: Burghotel – Kyffhäuser Post Rossla Harz Berlin SW 68. Date: 25.1.1944 Hedemannstraße 24
Ref: Sip. No. 140 29 1/Ko. Marriage permit of the SS (Paragraphs 13 Marriage law and 27 Military law)
The SS Oberscharführer Josef Rastädter born on 10.11.1914 in Werschetz (Banat) Serbia, resident at this time on the battlefield, has been granted permission to marry Miss Friedl Romagnoli, born on 10.11.1920 in Werschetz, resident in Budapest. The Certificates stating that there are no impediments to the marriage, have not been submitted. The certificates stating that there are no impediments to the marriage, issued by the health departments in accordance with the decree of the 23. 11. 1944 by the Reichs ministry R.M.Bliv. S 2299 have been granted. The authorisation necessary for members of the Waffen SS under Paragraph 27 of Military law, given by the relevant superior, is contained within this licence. The document's validity expires one year after its issue. The head of the Race and Settlement Office SS I.A. Piepko former SS-Oberscharführer S.L. The registrar is requested to send the attached 2nd part to the Reichsführer SS Race and Settlement Office Berlin SW 68 Hedemannstrasse 24, after it has been completed and signed. A return envelope is included. -------------------
L.Z. 73/1944
The copy prepared by me is authentic with the original, which was issued by the Head of the Race and Settlement Office SS on 25. 1. 1944 and was shown to me.
Werschetz, 21st twenty first March 1944 one thousand nine hundred and forty four.
Administration: 50.- Din.
Stamp duty: 30.- "
Together 80.- Dinar. Public Notary.

enststelle der
Feldpostnummer 13258

Im Felde, den 2o. Juli 1944

Frau

Luise Dümmer geb. Schroneborn

N o r d h o r n
===============
Ludwigstraße 56

Sehr geehrte Frau Dümmer!

Ich habe die traurige Pflicht, Ihnen mitteilen zu müssen, daß Ihr lieber Mann, der Gefreite Dietrich Dümmer, geboren am 9.12.o7 am 17. Juli 1944 gegen 2o Uhr auf unserem ptverbandsplatz verstorben ist, nachdem er am gleichen Tage durch einen Splitterdurchschlag im linken Oberschenkel mit Schussbruch und Zerreißung der Gefäße schwerst verwundet wurde. Trotz sofortiger Operation durch den besten Chirurgen unserer Division, bei der alle ärztliche Kunst und Mühe angewandt wurde, war es leider nicht möglich, daß fliehende Leben zu retten. Ihr Mann ist in bewustlosem Zustand, hervorgerufen durch den hohen Blutverlust, sanft entschlafen.

Ich spreche Ihnen zu dem schweren Verlust meine wärmste Anteilnahme aus.

Ihr Mann wurde auf dem kleinen Heldenfriedhof innerhalb des Gemeindefriedhofs in Simnas, etwa 100 m westlich der Dorfkirche an der Rollbahn Olita, lo km westlich Santaika und lo km ostwärts Krosna (1. Reihe Grab Nr. 5) unter militärischen Ehren beigesetzt.

Die vorgefundenen Nachlassgegenstände werden Ihnen zu gegebener Zeit von hier aus übersandt.

er den Ort und die näheren Umstände der Verwundung ist hier nichts bekannt, ich bitte Sie, sofoern Sie hierüber näheres erfahren wollen, sich mit dem Truppenteil Ihres gefallenen Mannes in Verbindung zu setzen.

Möge die Gewissheit, daß Ihr lieber Mann für die Größe und den Bestand von Volk, Führer und Reich sein Leben hingegeben hat, Ihnen ein Trost in dem schweren Leid sein, das Sie betroffen hat.

Ich grüße Sie in aufrichtigem Mitgefühl und mit Heil Hitler!

Oberstabsarzt u. Kp.-Chef

Die Richtigkeit vorstehender Abschrift
wird bescheinigt.
Hodenhagen, den 28.8.44
Der Bürgermeister:
i.A. Arnold

Gemeinde Hodenhagen Kreis Fallingbostel

Office Department for
Fieldpost number 13258

On the Battlefield, 20. July 1944

Frau

Luise Dümmer née Schroneborn

N o r d h o r n
===============
Ludwigstraße 56

Dear Mrs. Dümmer!

It is my sad duty to inform you that your dear husband, lance corporal Dietrich Dümmer,born 9.12.07, has passed away on 17th July 1944 at around 20.00 hours at our field hospital, after having been wounded on the same day by a splinter, which ripped his thigh, causing it to fracture and tearing the vessels. Despite being operated on immediately by the best surgeon of our division and with the best medical skills and effort being applied, it was not possible to save his life. Your husband was unconscious, due to the vast loss of blood, when he passed away peacefully.

I would like to offer you my deepest sympathy in your great loss.

Your husband was buried with military honours in the small war cemetery, which lies within the village cemetery, about 100m to the west of the village church (1st Row Grave No.5) The cemetery is situated near the runway Olite, which lies 10km to the west of Santaika and 10km to the east of Krosna.

The personal effects left behind will be sent to you from here in due course.

The place where your husband was injured, and the exact circumstances are not known to us here. If you would like to know more about it, please get in touch with the unit of your fallen husband.

May the certainty, that your dear husband has sacrificed his life for the long-lasting grandeur of the German Reich, its people and for the Führer, give you comfort in your sorrow which has befallen you.

Sending you my sincere sympathy and with Heil Hitler!

Senior Doctor & Company Commander

The authenticity of the above copy
is herewith confirmed
Hodenhagen 28.08.44

Mayor

This Kriegsmarine Oberleutnant zur See (Lieutenant) is wearing his frock coat in formal dress style, with shoulder straps rather than full dress with epaulettes. As is usual with formal dress, a bow tie is worn. He wears the Officers' gilt brocade belt, gold bullion breast eagle, 1939-1945 Iron Cross 1st and 2nd Class and an Armed Forces Long Service medal.

Note the floral sprig worn on his left breast lapel which indicates that he is 'God-fearing' (Christian faith).

A large formal group photograph in celebration of the marriage of an Oberleutnant zur See. He too, is wearing his "formal dress" uniform with Iron Cross 2nd Class and Long Service medal and has the floral sprig in his left lapel. Several other Kriegsmarine officers are present, perhaps shipmates, all of whom are wearing the Iron Cross 1st Class. Also pictured is a Luftwaffe aircrew officer wearing the Iron Cross 1st Class, the Pilot/Navigator badge and what would appear to be a Wound badge. Also, above his left breast pocket he wears the Bomber Clasp and several medal ribbons.

At top left, another officer guest is wearing the blue Reefer jacket, which was allowed for parades and walking-out, but not however, whilst in Berlin. He is an Oberleutnant zur See, but with engineering insignia replacing the normal star on his cuff and has also been awarded the Iron Cross 1st and 2nd Class. Below these we can see his High Seas Fleet badge. Note that he is wearing a normal tie with turndown shirt collar.

This proud father or grandfather is wearing his Kapitänleutnants' (Lieutenant-Commander) uniform, consisting of the summer white-topped Service Visor cap with gold bullion trim on the peak. The National Eagle insignia is in cast metal and the oak leaf wreath and cockade is embroidered gold bullion. His frock coat is in the "formal dress" style with gold bullion breast eagle and rank insignia on the cuffs, above which are his speciality/trade patches indicating Administration. The Officers' belt is the leather type with Officers' pressed gilt metal buckle. Hanging from his left side is his Offizierdolch (Officers' dagger).

Although we cannot see his rank, this Officer's Service Visor cap bullion indicates a rank of Leutnant zur See, Oberleutnant zur See, or Kapitänleutnant (Sub-Lieutenant, Lieutenant, or Lieutenant-Commander). His cap is the winter version in dark blue with woven gold bullion wreath and cockade. His blue Reefer jacket is decorated with the ribbons for the Iron Cross 1st and 2nd Class, below which can be seen his Submariners' badge. Around his neck is the Ritterkreuz des Eisernen Kreuzes (Knight's Cross of the Iron Cross).

This Bootmannsmaat (petty officer) is wearing his standard blue Jumper and blue Collar with stripes and a neckerchief (often referred to as a 'Silk') beneath the collar. The Other Ranks' breast eagle insignia is of yellow machine-embroidered thread and the medal bar is unclear. Below that is worn the Minesweeper badge and on his left arm is his rank badge, below are his red thread embroidered speciality/trade patches: Gunnery above and Ordnance (Mines) beneath.

This Obermaat (senior petty officer) is wearing the home waters (September to April) blue Brimless cap often nicknamed the Donald Duck cap, the band of which reads 'Kriegsmarine'. The National Eagle insignia is of pressed gilt. Earlier pre-war cap bands often carried the name of the ship or detachment to which the sailor belonged, before security became an issue. For summer, or whilst in the tropics, the cap top was white. His uniform jacket, peculiar to the Kriegsmarine was used for dress and summer walking out and carries the anchor and chevron denoting his rank in what appears to be pressed gilt metal. Above that, we see the Narvik campaign shield, indicating active service in Norway in 1940. On his left breast he wears the Iron Cross 2nd Class and below that, the Destroyer badge.

This young bridegroom is wearing his summer white-topped Brimless cap, the band of which probably reads Schiffsstammabteilung der Nordsee (Ship Home Department of the North Sea). His Uniform jacket carries his rank of sick berth petty officer. The lanyard indicates that he is a marksman, however the attached symbol denoting the area of expertise is hidden (an acorn for machine gunner/rifleman, a winged grenade for anti-aircraft machine gunner, a plain grenade for gunlayer or a torpedo for torpedo coxwains.

Another example of the Uniform jacket being worn over the white summer Jumper, this time showing it in full. Note the gold braid stripe on the cuff denoting petty officer rank. As with all petty officers' jackets, the breast eagle is of embroidered yellow silk. Unfortunately the badge of service on his left waist is obscured.

This engine room specialist wears his Laufbahn or speciality/trade badge on his upper left arm and below that, the three chevrons denoting his rank as Matrosenhauptgefreiter (leading seaman of 4.5 years' service or more). According to Kriegsmarine regulations, rank and trade badges are in yellow thread for the blue Jumper and in cornflower blue for the white summer Jumper, but when the Uniform jacket is worn, this insignia must be in gold bullion braid. Under his Uniform jacket he wears the white Jumper indicating that the marriage took place during the summer months.

A good shot of the blue Brimless cap with Kriegsmarine cap band (or tally ribbon), note the ribbon ends extending down over his shoulder. We can just see his striped Collar under his Pea jacket issued instead of a greatcoat for cooler weather. It could be worn, as here, over the Jumper or Uniform jacket. The same regulations apply for insignia as on the Uniform jacket in that they must be gold bullion braid. The plain cornflower-coloured collar patches and twin rank chevrons on his left arm indicate that he is a Matrosenobergefreiter (leading seaman) of less than 4.5 years' service. Above the chevrons is a specialty/trade badge for sick berth personnel.

This rather mature coastal artilleryman wears the standard Wehrmacht issue Model 43 field grey Field Service tunic, but with the addition of grey-green marine anchor buttons. On his shoulder straps are the yellow/gold machine-woven marine artillery insignia of winged ordnance and anchor. The Kriegsmarine breast eagle is also in yellow/gold thread and of the BeVo machine-woven type. His collar patches are for coastal artillery and are thin yellow stripes either side of a white bar.

Another example of the Uniform jacket being worn, but here there are no rank stripes on the buttoned cuff indicating that this young man is a Matrose (ordinary seaman). His Brimless cap has the summer white top and Kriegsmarine cap band.

This lower-deck rating is wearing his blue Brimless cap with pressed metal eagle insignia and cockade with the Kriegsmarine cap band woven, as per regulation, in flat gold thread. His Pea jacket carries the plain cornflower-blue collar patches and a rank star on his left sleeve. Unfortunately, we cannot see if he has rank chevrons below the star, which if not, would indicate his rank as Matrosengefreiter (able seaman). He has the sprig of flowers denoting his "God-fearing" religious belief and the ribbons of several awards, one of which is the Iron Cross 2nd Class.

An Oberleutnant of the Sonderführer (special task officer) wearing his Officers' Service Visor cap with silver bullion embroidered National Eagle and wreathed cockade with cap cords. His tunic, the Kleiner Dienstanzug für Kriegsverwaltungsbeamte (undress/informal uniform) is unadorned except for his Sonderführers' collar patches and his Eickhorn officers' dress sword with gilt guard and pommel with portepee.

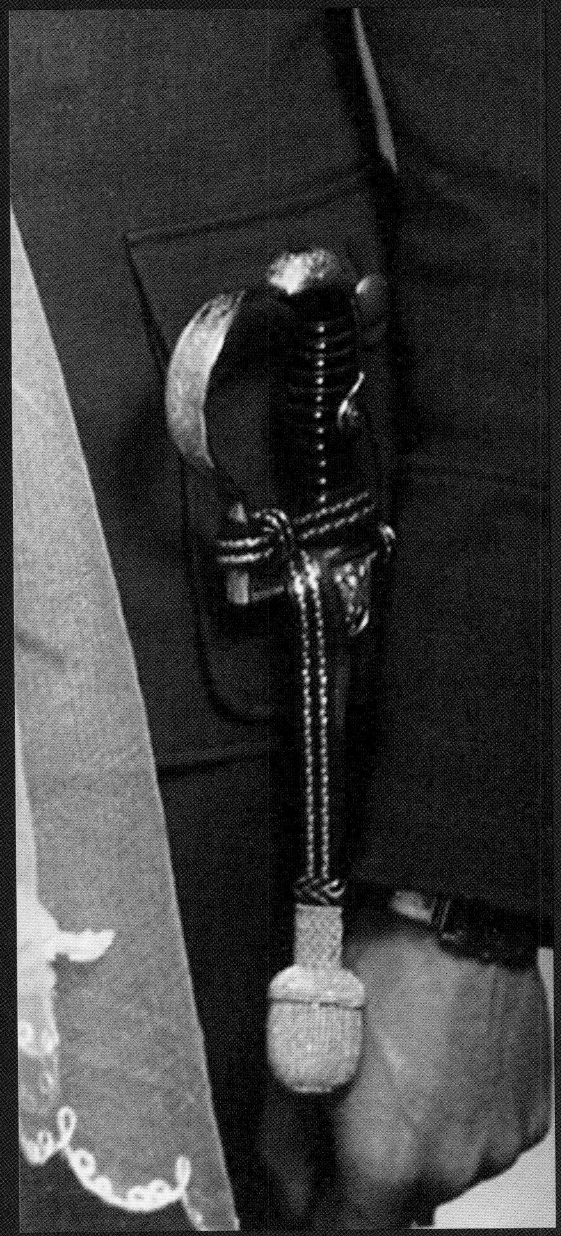

Another Sonderführer, but of Leutnant (2nd lieutenant) rank. His Officers' Service Visor cap carries pressed metal eagle and cockade insignia. His breast eagle is of embroidered silver bullion wire. His tunic is a variation of the undress uniform. Hanging from his left side is his army Officers' dagger with portepee.

This army Hauptmann (captain) is wearing his Officers' Service Visor cap with pressed metal insignia. His tunic is the piped field service pattern with the addition of silver parade aiguillettes. On his right breast is an Officers' bullion embroidered eagle and just visible on his left breast is a medal ribbon with the 1914-1918 Hindenburg War Service Cross.

This Oberleutnant (lieutenant) is wearing his Officers' Service Visor cap with pressed metal eagle and bullion embroidered wreathed cockade. The cap has had its wire stiffener removed to give it a more used aspect. His tunic is the service dress pattern, worn here as a form of dress uniform with aiguillettes and the Officers' green and silver brocaded belt. On his left breast are two unidentified medal ribbons, the Iron Cross 1st Class, General Assault badge and wound badge in black. His Officers' sword and portepee hang from his left side. Footwear appears to be riding boots with spurs.

The wedding of Leutnant von Westerhagen. Unusually he is wearing his model 1935 steel helmet with the army eagle transfer on the left side. His uniform is the piped Field Service tunic with the addition of his Officers' brocade belt. His Officers' sword is at his side and his boots are worn with spurs. The lady congratulating them is wearing the uniform of a Red Cross nurse. In the background can be seen one of Westerhagen's fellow-officers, also wearing the Service Uniform with brocade belt, but with aiguillettes.

Another photograph of the same newlyweds. We can see more clearly, his piped Field Service tunic adorned with the Iron Cross 2nd Class and Winter Campaign in the East medal. Below these are his Ground Assault and wound badge, which is possibly in silver. A gold wound badge would suggest a fairly devastating injury. A good view of his brocade belt is afforded, as is his Officers' sword portepee.

This army officer is also wearing his double insignia model 1935 steel helmet (eagle shield on the left and National shield on the right side) for his wedding. His tunic is the Full Dress Uniform with decorated bullion cuffs and collar patches, aiguillettes and brocade belt. His medals include the Iron Cross 2nd Class and a service medal. He wears a floral sprig denoting his religious belief and carries an Officers' sword with portepee at his side.

This young Leutnant is wearing his Weisserrock (white tunic) without a belt. He appears to have a pressed-metal eagle on his right breast and a floral sprig on his pocket. His medals include his Iron Cross 2nd Class and Winter Campaign in the East. Below that is his Iron Cross 1st Class, General Assault and wound badges. His Service Visor cap has an embroidered bullion National Eagle and wreathed cockade insignia and the piping is a dark colour. He holds the programme of the service which carries a crucifix on the reverse. His Officers' sword and portepee are held in his left hand.

This older officer wears his model 1938 Feldmütze (field cap). It has an officers flat-weave eagle, possibly in silver wire with a Soutache (inverted 'V' piping) over the embroidered national cockade. The cap also carries officers' silver bullion piping around the crown and flap. His tunic looks to be a privately-purchased Service Uniform with shoulder boards of Leutnant rank and regimental number 103 or 105 in pressed metal numerals. One of the medal ribbons is possibly the World War I Hindenburg Cross with Swords and below that on his breast pocket is the World War I Iron Cross and World War I wound badge. We have a good view of his Officers' double-clawed brown leather belt.

Another, more mature officer with his family. His elder son is a Kriegsmarine rating and is wearing his Pea jacket. The younger son is in the marine Hitler Jugend and wears his enamel HJ badge and brassard over his blue Kriegsmarine Jumper. Their father is an army Leutnant and is wearing his full dress uniform with aiguillettes. Like the preceding officer, he too is a veteran of World War I and wears his Iron Cross Second Class, the Prussian officers' Long Service medal and the Honour or Hindenburg Cross with Swords. Below that is his World War I Iron Cross First Class, which is convex and has a screw-back fixing. Also visible is a World War I wound badge.

This Leutnant is wearing his Field Service tunic with piping around the edges. His breast eagle is embroidered bullion and he has his Iron Cross 2nd Class ribbon in his buttonhole. His Iron Cross 1st Class is pinned on his left breast pocket, below that, his General Assault and black wound badges. His trousers also have his Waffenfarbe (arm of service piping) running down the side of each leg.

■ Another young Leutnant in his piped Field Service tunic. His shoulder boards carry a pressed metal Lyre motif signifying that he is a musician from the army school of music. His medals are the Iron Cross 2nd Class, the Winter Campaign in the East and Annexation of the Sudetenland with Prague Castle Bar. Just visible below is the Iron Cross 1st Class.

■ This Oberleutnant wears his Undress uniform with the addition of his Officers' brocade belt. His shoulder boards carry his regimental number in pressed metal and his awards above his left breast pocket are the Iron Cross 2nd Class and Westwall medals. Below that are the Iron Cross 1st Class, a wound badge in black and an Infantry Assault badge.

This Leutnant is a medical officer which is signified by a pressed metal staff of Asclepius (a serpent entwined around a staff) on his shoulder boards. His officers' Service uniform is adorned with a bullion embroidered breast eagle, which is clearly illustrated, as is the black backing cloth it is woven onto.

These NCOs seem intent on taking a rather anxious-looking lady for a spin in their BMW R12 motorcycle and sidecar combination. Both men at the rear are wearing the model 1936 Service tunic. The man on the left is of sergeant-major rank and has pointed, early pattern shoulder straps and a flat machine-woven breast eagle on a light grey backing cloth. Both NCOs sport the early saucer-shape ORs' Service Visor cap, one with motorcycle despatch riders' goggles. He also wears high leather marching boots. The driver wears a waterproof rubberised motorcycle coat and also has goggles. All indications point to this being a pre-war photograph.

This Obergerfreiter wears his Full Dress uniform with Service Visor cap. Just visible is his numbered regimental shoulder strap. At the top of his sleeves are his Swalbeennester (swallows' nests) which show him to be a military musician and by various colours, the branch of service he might belong to. This traditional item of dress was worn by four categories of musician: drummers, pipers, trumpeters and buglers. His rank chevrons are below the swallows' nest and we can see that he has been awarded several medals and a wound badge which is probably in silver. His breast eagle is flat woven onto a black backing and from his right shoulder hangs a marksmanship lanyard.

This veteran NCO is wearing his Service Visor cap with pressed metal eagle, but with a bullion embroidered cockade. His tunic is the Full Dress version for NCOs with his shoulder straps indicating his rank as Unteroffzier (junior sergeant). His medals are the Iron Cross 2nd Class, the Winter Campaign in the East, the Army Service medal, the Annexation of Czechoslovakia medal and Westwall Defence medal. Below those is pinned his Iron Cross 1st Class. His Officers' dress sword with portepee is the lion's head version which is set with rubies.

Another Unteroffizier in his Full Dress uniform. He wears a floral sprig on his tunic under which is his army service and Westwall medals. Below those is his DRL sports badge. He too carries the lion's-head version of the Officers' Dress sword. His Service Visor cap has pressed-metal insignia.

A very fine wedding portrait, which shows a Feldwebel in his Full Dress uniform. He too wears a floral sprig and has the Annexation of Czechoslovakia and army service medals. He wears his ORs' leather belt and white metal buckle with the chains from his sword hanger just visible. The Officers' Dress sword is worn here, unhooked and held in his white-gloved hand. His ORs' Service Visor cap carries dark arm of service piping around its crown.

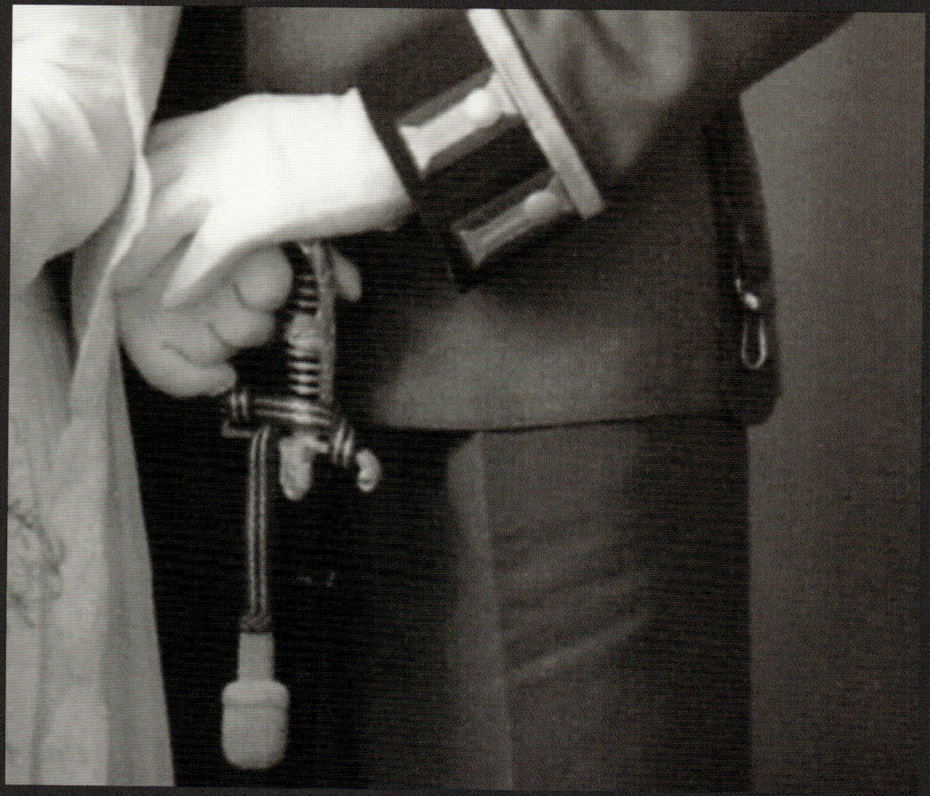

Another really nice photograph of a 'happy couple'. This Oberfeldwebel (sergeant-major) with two pips on his shoulder straps, also has pressed-metal insignia on his Service Visor cap. His Full Dress uniform has many awards attached. On his left breast is the Nahenkampfesabzeichen (close combat clasp) in bronze, below that his Iron Cross 2nd Class, his Winter Campaign in the East medal and the Austrian Anschluss medal and either Sudetentland or Memel medal. Under those are his Iron Cross 1st Class and floral sprig, his wound badge in black and his SA sports badge. His Officers' Dress sword is also unhooked, and his sword hanger is of leather.

A Feldwebel wearing his Full Dress uniform with collar Tresse and marksmanship lanyard. His breast eagle is flat-woven bullion wire and he appears to have an army service medal next to his floral sprig. On each shoulder strap is a pressed metal regimental numeral just above his rank pip and his ORs' Service Visor cap also has pressed metal insignia and a wire crown stiffener. At his left side can be seen his NCOs' Dress sword and portepee.

A good, clear photograph of a newly-married Red Cross nurse, standing beside her husband, wearing her enamel badge. The groom is a Gefreiter and is wearing his 1936 pattern Walking Out uniform. In his buttonhole is his Winter Campaign in the East award and on his left sleeve his rank chevrons. His ORs' Service Visor cap is nicely shaped with the stiffening wire removed. The insignia is pressed white metal.

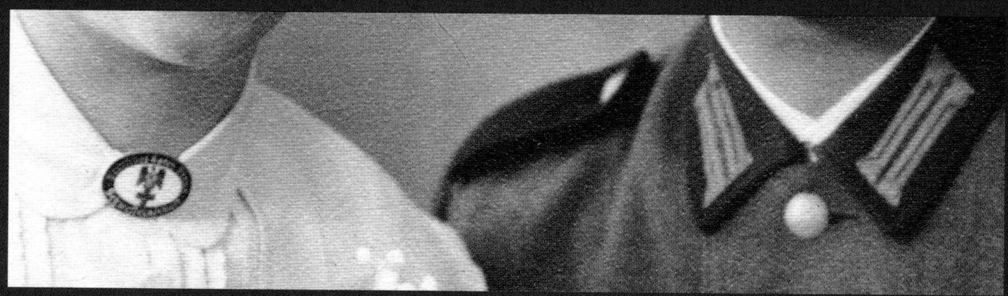

This youthful, veteran campaigner is an Unteroffizier and is wearing his model 1936 Service uniform with dark green collar worn open. The tunic appears to have been shortened, possibly to improve freedom of movement. On it he has his breast eagle which looks to be the flat machine-woven wire variety. In his buttonhole is his Iron Cross 2nd Class ribbon and on his left breast pocket his wound badge in black and his Infantry Assault badge. On his upper left arm is the Krim (Crimea) Shield identifying him as having participated in the difficult assault on the Black Sea ports around Sevastopol in the Soviet Union. His Service Visor cap is the regulation ORs' type with patent leather chinstrap. His ORs' leather belt carries a white metal buckle, here, possibly silver-washed. Note the issue field grey woollen gloves.

This Gefreiter also wears his 1936 pattern Walking Out uniform with coloured Waffenfarbe (arm of service piping) around his shoulder straps and his Service Visor cap, which has its wire stiffener in place. On his left sleeve we see his rank chevrons and on his left breast pocket the War Merit Cross with Swords in bronze.

This Feldwebel is wearing the regulation ORs' Service Visor cap with metal eagle and wreathed cockade and with a patent leather chinstrap. His tunic, however, seems to be a form of piped Full Dress uniform, but without the 'Swedish'-style braided cuff facings nor belt. His early pattern marksmanship lanyard has two acorns attached, signifying him as having won the award twice successively. On his left breast is his army service medal and DRL sports badge. His NCOs' Dress sword hangs from his left hip.

This Gefreiter (corporal) is wearing his Service Visor cap and 1943 pattern Service tunic, differing in detail from the model 1936 by the colour of the collar and shoulder boards (from dark green to field-grey). However this particular tunic retains the box pleated pockets and three-point flaps of the model 1936. The breast eagle is of a flat machine-woven type, grey on a field grey backing. His rank chevron is on his left sleeve and his ribbon could be either the Westwall or Social Welfare medal. His NCOs' Dress sword with portepee is held in his left hand, but is still attached to its leather hangers. We can just see the support hooks on his tunic, that carry his leather ORs' belt. His bride wears a black wedding dress with white veil, traditional in some parts of Germany until after the war.

Here we see an Unteroffizier (junior sergeant) acting as a Spiess (senior sergeant) who would run the company H.Q. and supervise all disciplinary matters. A Speiss would normally have the rank of Hauptfeldwebel with two rank pips on his shoulder straps. He sits beside his bride on their wedding day, being driven to the church in a flower-draped carriage. His ORs' Service Visor cap retains its wire stiffener and has a very high crown. The National Eagle and wreathed cockade insignia is of pressed white metal. He wears the 1936 Service uniform and has what might be a cavalry sabre on his left hip. He wears the Iron Cross 2nd Class ribbon and another award, possibly the Winter Campaign in the East medal, in his buttonhole. Over to the right of the ribbons on his breast pocket is another curiosity, which appears to be a model of a bird sitting on a hoop.

A very modern marriage couple pictured here, with a good detail of the ORs' Service Visor cap. All the component parts are quite clear, the Waffenfarbe (arm of service piping), the white metal National Eagle and wreathed cockade, the patent leather chinstrap and even the texture of the woollen crown. Also in good detail is his silver bullion-braided collar on his Full Dress uniform.

This Unteroffizier is also wearing his Full Dress uniform. His breast eagle is embroidered silver bullion wire on a black wool backing. His medal ribbon bar carries the War Merit Cross with Swords and the Winter Campaign in the East medals. Just below those is his floral sprig. His Service Visor cap retains its wire crown stiffener and almost completely masks his NCOs' Dress sword.

A double wedding here, with various Wehrmacht guests. All are Unteroffiziers with the exception of the man on the right who may be a junior NCO. The military guests are all wearing their 1936 Service uniforms and Service Visor caps except the man in the middle background who is wearing his Feldmütze (field service cap) with arm of service Soutache (an inverted 'V') over the cockade. The groom on the left has the Iron Cross 2nd Class hanging from his buttonhole and various other award ribbons on a bar on his left breast. Both grooms are wearing floral sprigs signifying their 'God-fearing' belief.

This Feldwebel's shoulder straps carry his rank pip, regiment number, and his field service insignia. His Full Dress uniform has a breast eagle in silver bullion thread, a marksman's lanyard, an army service medal on his left breast and below that his Deutshcher Reichsbund fur Leibesubungen (DRL) sports badge. In his hand he holds his NCOs' Dress sword detached from its leather hanger. His ORs' Service Visor cap is shown with its wire stiffener in place.

This Obergefreiter is wearing his 1943 pattern Service uniform to his wedding. It has pleated pockets, which suggests a late war date for the photograph. Of note is his ORs' leather belt with its field-grey painted buckle. He wears the General Assault badge on his left breast and has his trousers tucked into his high marching boots and blousoned. In his left hand he holds his NCOs' Sevice Visor cap with pressed metal insignia and suede gloves.

This young Gefreiter is wearing his standard pattern army field grey greatcoat with field grey collar. His cap is the 1943 Einheitsfeldmütze (general issue field cap) which derived its shape from caps worn by German troops serving in North Africa. It has a two-button flap and the National Eagle and cockade insignia is flat woven onto a trapezoid backing patch. Just visible on the left side of the cap is a badge, probably that of a Gebirgsjäger (mountain trooper), Skijäger (ski trooper) or Jäger (hunter).

This Oberfeldwebel is wearing his 1943 Einheitsfeldmütze with trapezoid insignia patch. His tunic is the 1943 Service type with pleated pockets. He has several medal ribbons above his floral sprig. Below that is his DRL sports and Infantry Assault badges. Note the patent leather belt and nickel-plated ORs' pressed metal buckle.

This very smart Unteroffizier is also wearing his 1943 Einheitsfeldmütze with trapezoid insignia patch. His breast eagle is quite bright and would suggest that this tunic was used for more formal occasions. The Winter Campaign in the East ribbon bar is above his left breast pocket and below is his wound, Infantry Assault and DRL sports badges. He too wears a patent leather ORs' belt. His trousers are tucked into his boots with his socks rolled over the top in the manner of the Gebirgsjäger (mountain troops).

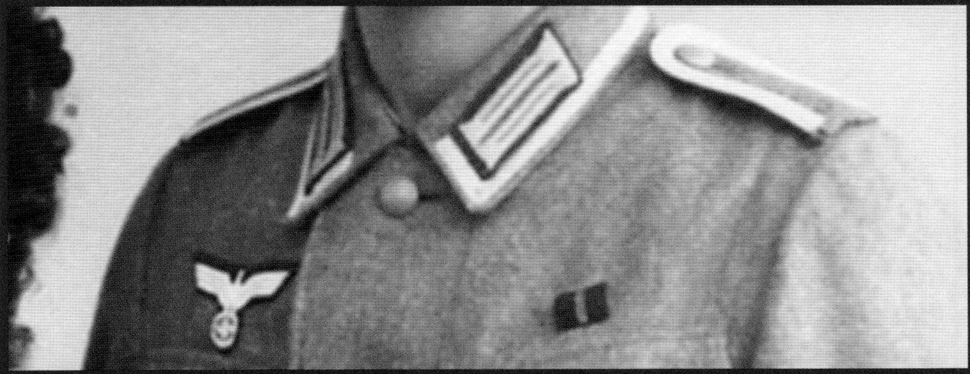

This Gefreiter wears his 1943 pattern Field Service tunic with rank chevrons on the arm. The eagle insignia on his right breast pocket is flat woven on a dark field-grey backing. His medal ribbons in his buttonhole are the Iron Cross 2nd Class and his Winter Campaign in the East medal. He has a floral sprig above the left breast pocket and a black wound badge below. The buckle on his ORs' belt is painted matt field grey. The cap he wears is the model 1942 ORs' Feldmütze with flat woven insignia.

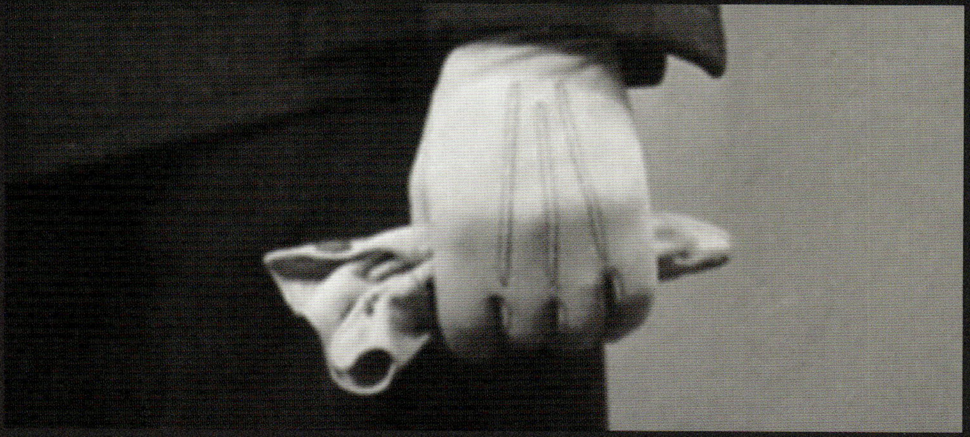

■ This Feldwebel, wearing his Full Dress uniform, has a floral sprig and DRL sports badge on his left breast. Note the absence of the National Eagle insignia, which must date this marriage as circa 1933. One of their guests is a SS-Scharführer (sergeant) in the Allegemeine-SS. His shirt and tie are brown and he has an enamel NSDAP membership badge pinned to it. On his left arm is the swastika brassard and below that an unidentified circular speciality/trade badge.

A very clear photograph of a Feldwebel wearing a rather splendid Full Dress uniform. We are afforded a good view of the 'Swedish' cuffs and brocaded collar. On his breast is an army service medal and what could be a Social Welfare medal. Below are his DRL and SA sports badges. His NCOs' dress sword and portepee hang from his side.

This Feldwebel, flanked by two comrades, also Feldwebels, is wearing his NCOs' Full Dress uniform with 'Swedish' brocade cuffs. His two comrades seem to be wearing a different version of the Dress uniform, that is, without the 'Swedish' cuffs. The breast eagles on these uniforms are more muted than the one on the groom's tunic and are woven onto a lighter backing patch.

Here an Oberfeldwebel (sergeant-major) wears his Full Dress uniform. On his breast is an army service medal and an Anschluss award for either the Sudetenland, Austria or Memel. On his right breast is a silver bullion thread embroidered eagle on a dark, probably black woollen backing.

This NCO is wearing his 1936 pattern Service tunic with NCO Tresse. His sleeve insignia of two silver bands indicate that he is a Spiess (senior sergeant). His medals include the War Merit Cross with Swords in bronze, the Winter Campaign in the East and the Sudetenland Anschluss. Below those is a DRL sports badge and wound badge in black.

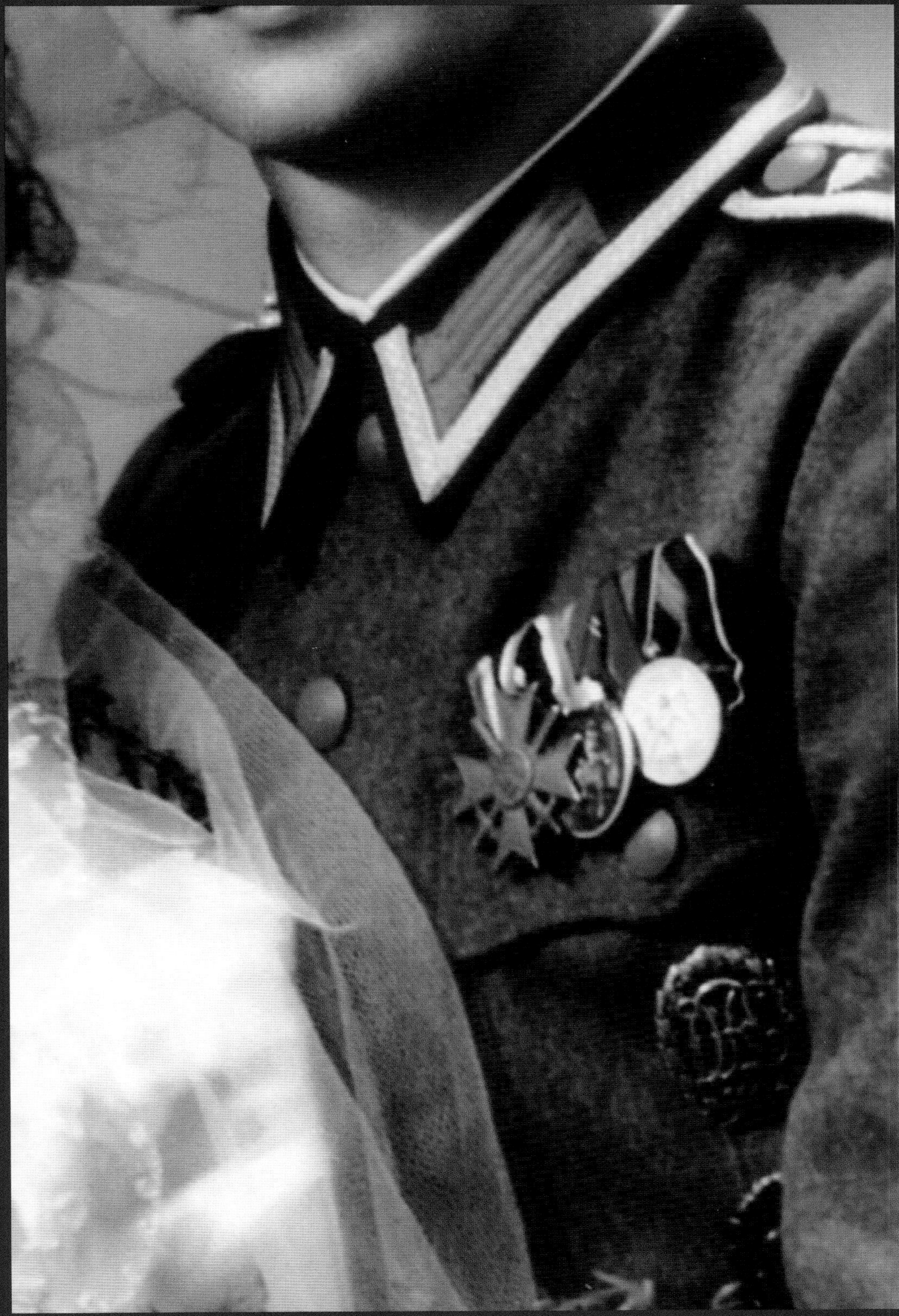

This bareheaded Gefreiter, his bride and their fathers were photographed in the second half of the war. His uniform is the 1942 pattern Service tunic with rank chevron on his left sleeve. His breast eagle insignia is flat-woven field grey on a grey backing and he has a wound badge probably black, now with the paint worn away, on his left breast pocket. His arm of service piping is clearly visible, running around his shoulder boards. The man on the right has a gold NSDAP enamel badge on his lapel.

Pictured in the Schattwald in 1944, Mr. and Mrs. Almer pose for the camera. He is an Oberfeldwebel and is wearing the reed-green denim field service tunic. He has the Iron Cross 2nd Class ribbon in his button hole and two medal ribbons on his left breast: the War Merit Cross with Swords and the Winter Campaign in the East. Below those is his SA sports badge and whistle lanyard. On his left arm is the Krim (Crimea) Shield. He wears cotton drill breeches tucked into high marching boots.

This unusual tinted photograph shows an Unteroffizier (junior sergeant) with an embroidered regimental number on his early style shoulder straps. His Service tunic is the 1936 pattern with dark green collar. His religious floral sprig appears to be attached to an unidentified medal ribbon.

■ This Obergefreiter wears his model 1936 service tunic with the dark green collar. On his shoulder strap is a slip-on regimental number of 171 which was part of the 115th Infantry Division. His breast eagle is the 1935 pattern flat-woven light grey on a dark green backing. The regulation ORs' leather belt and white metal buckle and rank chevrons complete the picture.

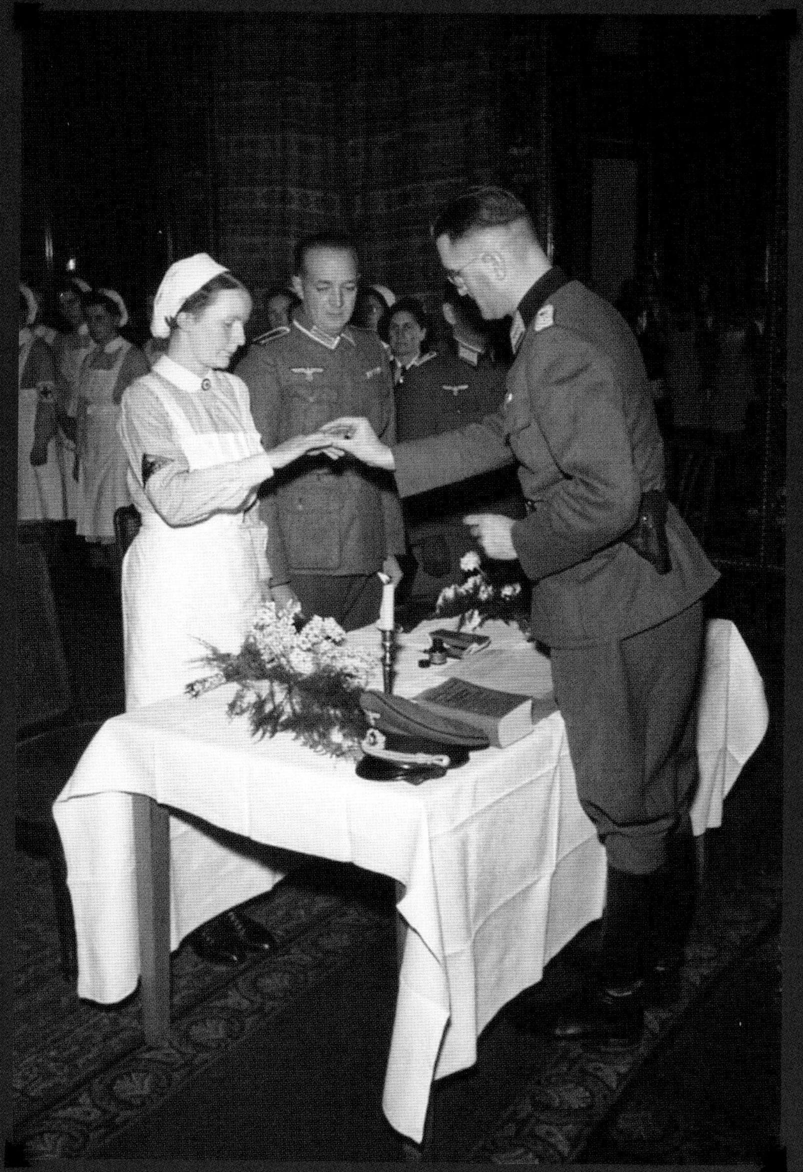

The first in a series of three photographs depicting the wedding of an army Unteroffizier to a Red Cross nurse. An army major is placing the ring on her finger. His Service tunic carries the Officers' leather belt from which hangs his brown leather PPK/PP holster and pistol. His Officers' Service Visor cap lies on the marriage table, showing dark arm of service piping, a metal National Eagle with bullion embroidered wreathed cockade and Officers' cap cords.

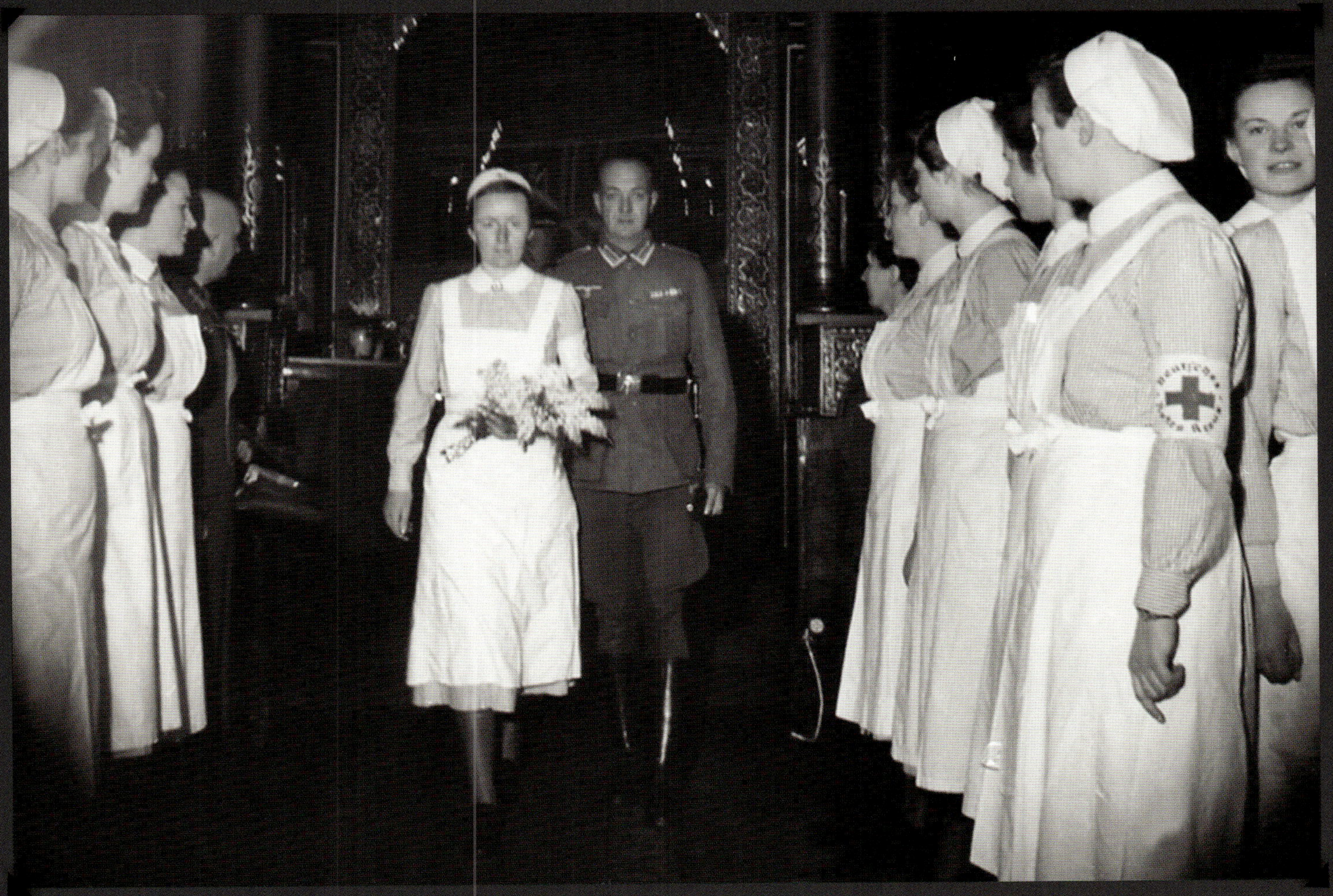

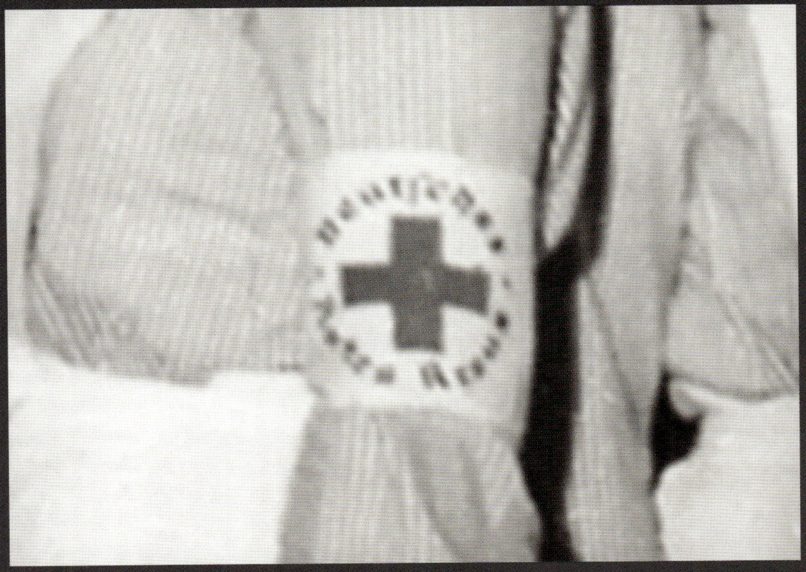

■ The wedding takes place in a soldiers' Red Cross hospital in St. Dizier, France. The newlywed couple pass down an honour guard of nurses who are all wearing regulation dresses and aprons with the nurses' Red Cross enamel badge pinned at the throat. On their left arm is the Red Cross brassard that reads, "Deutsches Rotes Kreuz". The groom is wearing his 1943 Service tunic with breeches tucked into high marching boots. A bayonet hangs from his ORs' belt on the left side. Numerous medal ribbons adorn his tunic signifying that he has 'been around'. In his left hand we can just see his Feldmütze with National Eagle and cockade insignia.

Obviously an affair of some importance, the guests to their wedding feast include several Red Cross officers of indeterminate rank. Their uniforms are coloured slate-grey and the collar insignia is on a dove-grey field with an enamel red cross at the centre and twisted bullion thread around the edge of the patch. The Red Cross officer with the moustache has service bars on his left sleeve indicating length of service. He also wears an enamel NSDAP badge on his left breast pocket. The bald officer on the right has many medal ribbons and orders on his breast, unfortunately unknown, but on his left sleeve is what appears to be the medical speciality/trade patch depicting the snake and staff of Asclepius. Asclepius was the legendary son of the Greek god Apollo, who learned the art of healing from the centaur Chiron.

This poor Unteroffizier has been knocked about a bit. His forehead bears the scars of quite a nasty wound, as confirmed by his silver or gold wound badge on his left breast pocket next to his General Assault badge, which although seemingly gold or silver, has no 25, 50, 75 or 100 engagement number at it's base and therefore is probably just highly polished or a privately-purchased item. He too wears a floral sprig and above that his Iron Cross 2nd Class, the Winter Campaign in the East and the Westwall Defence medals. His marksmanship lanyard is the later pattern, no longer just an eagle on a shield, but revised to an eagle above crossed swords over a shield. He wears the 1936 pattern service tunic in open collar style and post-1940 pattern rounded shoulder straps.

This rather romantic Unteroffizier is wearing his model 1936 Service tunic. We are afforded a sharp view of his collar patches and NCOs' Tresse. His shoulder straps carry his arm of service piping around the edge. His breast eagle is flat machine-woven white on a grey backing with what seems to be a further backing patch of dark green or black.

■ Another example of a 'proxy' marriage, where one of the partners is not present at the same ceremony. Our groom is wearing his model 1935 or 1940 issue stahlhelm (steel helmet). He has Feldwebel shoulder straps (with a single pip) on his model 1936 Service tunic. In his buttonhole is the ribbon for the Iron Cross 2nd Class and Winter Campaign in the East medals. His breast eagle is flat machine-woven grey on a grey-green backing and he has a Geprüftes-Hufbeschlagpersonal (qualified farriers') speciality/trade badge on his right forearm. Watched by his peers, two officers preside over the ceremony, in front of them sits a garlanded portrait of the bride.

This Schutze (private) wears his Full Dress uniform with a flat-woven bullion eagle on a grey-green backing. His ORs' belt buckle has been painted grey. His ORs' Service Visor cap is in pristine condition and has pressed white metal National Eagle with wreathed cockade insignia and patent leather chinstrap. On his shoulder strap is his regimental number '9'. The 9th Infantry regiment was also known as the 'Potsdam' or in a more derisory manner, the 'Graf Neun' as a large percentage of officers belonged to the aristocracy. Its other, more serious claim to fame was that nineteen of its officers were involved in the 20th July bomb plot to kill Hitler, most of whom were executed. Romantic as this photograph may seem, this could well be a propaganda studio shot, produced for the postal card market.

Another army Schutze, but wearing his 1943 Service tunic without pleated pockets. His flat-woven grey eagle on its field grey backing is the only insignia it bears, apart from his religious floral sprig. His ORs' Service Visor cap seems to be a lighter shade of grey than normal and made from doeskin rather than the usual wool (possibly privately- purchased).

Could this be the perfect National Socialst family? Father is wearing his 1936 Service tunic with the dark green collar. His flat-woven breast eagle is white on a dark green backing. His belt is the regulation ORs' type, being leather with a white metal buckle. He holds his Field Service cap which has a flat-woven National Eagle and cockade insignia. His sons are all Hitler Jugend (Hitler Youth) and are wearing their brown shirts with leather toggles and black neckerchiefs, leather belts with cross-straps and triangular HJ-Gebeite (Hitler Youth districts) insignia on their upper left arms. Black shorts were regulation wear as were long grey socks and black shoes. The eldest also wears his HJ brassard on his left sleeve. Mother sits contentedly amid her brood, another child and she would qualify for The Mothers' Cross in bronze for producing four to five children.

Here is another example of the 1943 Service tunic, but one with pleated pockets. We see his collar patches and breast eagle in good detail. The breast eagle is flat-woven grey thread on darker green or grey backing. He wears his model 1943 Einheitzfeldmütze (general issue Field cap) with two grey-painted buttons on the flap and the insignia is two-piece, a flat-woven National Eagle and separate cockade.

This Oberschutze (senior private) wears his Field Service cap with National Eagle and cockade insignia and the Soutache (an inverted 'V') in arm of service piping. His tunic is the 1943 pattern with pleated pockets and his straight trousers are tucked into his high marching boots. On his upper left arm is the rank insignia of a single woven pip on a black circular woollen patch.

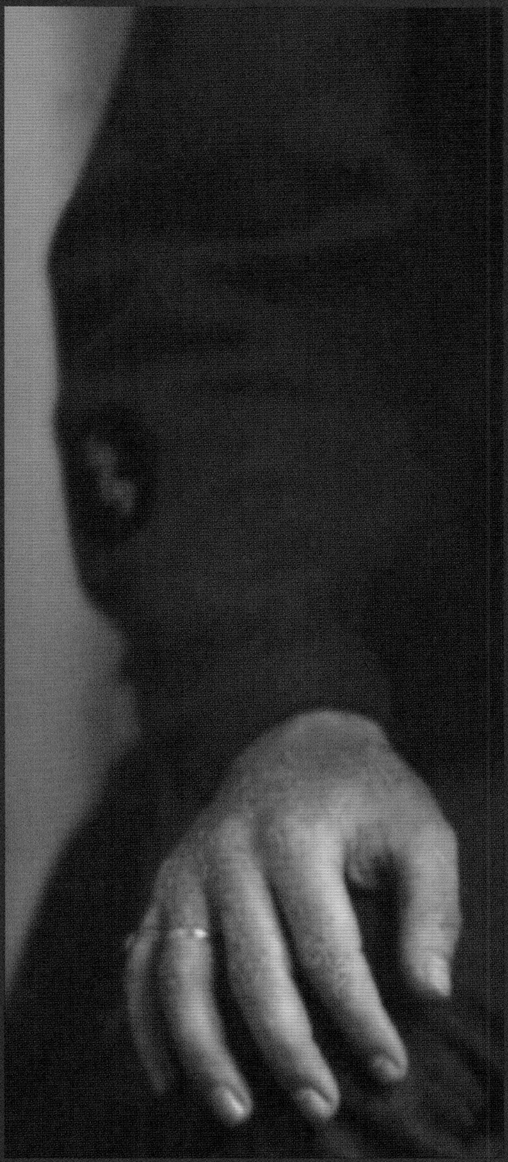

This new father of Schutze rank is also wearing his Field Service cap with dark Soutache. His tunic is the model 1936 and he has what looks like a Westwall defence ribbon on his left breast. On his right forearm is the Sanitätspersonal (medical personnel) speciality/trade badge.

This Schutze is wearing his standard pattern ORs' greatcoat with dark blue-green collar which was worn by troops of all ranks up to, but not including general. His Field Service cap also has a dark Soutache and separate flat-woven eagle and cockade insignia.

This young Schutze wears a variation of the greatcoat, of which there are at least thirteen varieties. This 1943 version has a large collar in the same, poor quality material as the coat. He wears dark woollen shoulder straps rather than the more usual grey and his ORs' leather belt with pressed metal buckle is worn over the coat.

This extremely young recruit is wearing what is probably his father's model 1936 Service tunic with whistle lanyard and cords. His model 1935/40 steel helmet rests so heavily on his head it appears to be forcing him down into his dad's high marching boots!

This member of the Panzertruppen is wearing the Panzer Schutzmütze (protective cap) which was introduced with the black armoured vehicle uniform in 1934. The black woollen beret carries a flat machine-woven separate National Eagle and wreathed cockade in white thread on a black backing. Inside the beret is a padded crash helmet.

His Panzerjacke (tank tunic) is the first pattern and known as the 'panzer wrapover' as the front left lapel can be buttoned up over the right breast for added warmth. The collar patches are black with a pressed metal skull, signifying armoured troops and is piped in arm of service colours (here, probably pink for armour, although golden-yellow for reconnaissance was the other variation). His shirt is either grey or buff and the tie is black. The ORs' belt and buckle is also worn and the trousers have button-down flap pockets and are blousoned into high ankle-length leather boots.

Here we see the same man shown on the previous page, with his bride. He now wears the later black panzer Field Service cap introduced in 1940. The tunic is probably the same one as before, but now has his Winter Campaign in the East medal ribbon in his breast buttonhole and Gefreiter rank chevrons on his left sleeve. The portrait on the right affords us a good view of his collar patches and Field Service cap which has flat machine-woven insignia and a Soutache of pink Waffenfarbe (arm of service piping).

■ This Panzer officer is wearing the Field Service cap with officers' silver bulllion piping around the crown and flap. The insignia is probably a flat weave, but may well be in silver bullion thread rather than ORs' white cotton. His Leutnant's shoulder boards are also bullion cord and his tunic is the regulation Panzerjacke.

Not strickly speaking a 'panzer man' this Gefreiter belongs to a Sturmgeschütz (assault gun) unit. Their uniforms, while being the same cut as the black panzer outfit, are in field grey material. He retains the pressed metal skull collar patches, but on grey backing and he has a silver wound badge and probably a General Assault badge. His belt buckle is painted a drab grey and his shirt and tie are also grey. His Field Service cap is the same as the black panzer version but again, in field grey. His button-down flap pocket trousers are blousoned, but into ankle boots and his gloves are the issue grey woollen type. They pose outside the registry office for the region of Berlin-Steglitz.

This Sturmgeschütz NCO is also wearing his field grey wrapover tunic. The shoulder straps, which are piped red for artillery, tell us he is a Feldwebel and has the ribbons for the Iron Cross 2nd Class and Winter Campaign in the East medals in his left lapel button hole, below that is his Iron Cross 1st Class. His right breast eagle is flat machine-woven white thread on a dark green backing. Not all Sturmgeschütz personnel wore the panzer skull collar patches, as evidenced here with the use of 'Litzen' patches, as used by most army units. His shirt is grey and his tie black.

This Sturmgeschütz crew member also has 'Litzen'-style collar patches on his field grey Panzerjacke, rather than the panzer skulls. He has a slip-on over his shoulder boards with a woven number "1" (possibly StuG.Abt.1 der Luftwaffe, which was part of 1. Fallschirm. Korps). Unfortunately we cannot see his breast eagle to determine if it is army or air force, nor his model 1943 Einheitsfeldmütze. On his left arm are his Obergefreiter rank chevrons. He has a floral sprig above his medals which include the Iron Cross 2nd Class, the Winter Campaign in the East, the Memel, Sudeten or Austrian Anschluss medal and below, a black wound badge. His trousers are blousoned and tucked into his low-cut marching boots.

This and the following photograph depict another 'proxy' marriage, this time the groom is from the Panzertruppen. Behind him sit four fellow panzermen, the man on the far left being an officer, probably his C.O. (he wears the officers' belt and a two-pronged buckle over his black Panzerjacke. He also wears leather gloves and has a Panzerkampfabzeichen (tank assault badge) on his lower left breast, as does the panzer trooper behind the army officer wearing a model 1936 Service tunic.

The groom and his commanding officer watch as his comrades witness the marriage document. From this angle we can see the groom has Gefreiter rank chevrons, as does his other witness. As the man at centre bends over to sign the document placed over the swastika-draped table, we can see a leather 'hardshell' Luger holster that he wears on his belt. A portrait of Adolf Hitler lies on the desk beside the vase of flowers.

This panzerman is wearing the Panzerjacke with skull collar patches (after January 1943 the wearing of the skull collar patches was forbidden for non-tank personnel, they would all have to wear Litzen-style patches. Our groom has Obergefreiter rank chevrons on his sleeve, a floral sprig and the ORs' black leather belt and pressed white metal buckle.

In this other photograph of the same newlyweds, we get a better view of his headdress and tunic. His cap is the black panzer model 1943 with a two-button flap and flat machine-woven insignia, which appears to be flat-woven onto a 'T'-shaped black backing. His cap buttons are painted black. His collar patches, shoulder boards and rank chevrons are clearly shown, as is his silky black tie on a white shirt. Under his floral sprig we can see his Winter Campaign in the East medal ribbon in his buttonhole.

Although not perhaps strictly a panzerman, this Leutnant is a member of the 3rd Company Anti-tank Battalion 616. His Stamroll number was '4' and his blood group 'A' as we see from his Erkennungsmarke (identity disc). At his wedding he is wearing his Officers' Full Dress uniform with aiguillettes and Officers' brocade belt. In his left hand he holds his Officers' Dress sword with lion's-head motif and portepee. The Waffenfarbe around his shoulder boards, Litzen-style collar patches and his Officers' Service visor cap are pink for Panzertruppen.

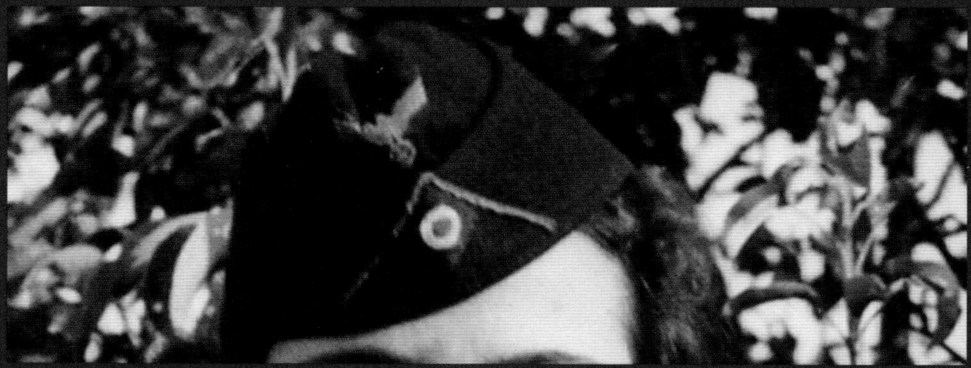

It was not at all uncommon for sweethearts or wives to dress up in their partner's uniform for a souvenir photograph. Here a young lady is wearing her beau's black Panzerjacke. The breast eagle is flat machine-woven in white thread on a black backing. On her left breast are a tank assault and a DRL sports badge. Her cap is the black Panzer Field Service (forage) type with flat machine-woven insignia and a coloured Soutache over the cockade.

Another example of the bride wearing black. Her husband is in his tan-coloured Tropical Field Service uniform with straight-leg trousers and shoes. He has Obergefreiter rank chevrons on his arm and a tan tropical canvas ORs' belt. His cap is the Deutsches Afrikakorps Feldmütze in tan, which was the forerunner of the model 1943 Einheitsfeldmütze.

This Obergefreiter is also wearing the Deutsches Afrikakorps Feldmütze. The National Eagle insignia is flat-woven blue-grey on a copper-brown backing. The cockade, also flat-woven, is on the same backing colour. His greatcoat is the Afrikakorps khaki type and has rank chevrons on the left sleeve. His model 84/98 bayonet hangs from his ORs' belt and his boots are the high, front lacing, canvas and leather tropical pattern.

The happy father of this family is wearing his ORs' Service Visor cap with pressed white metal National Eagle insignia and wreathed cockade. Between the two insignia is a metal Edelweiss badge which singles him out as a Gebirgsjäger (mountain trooper). His tunic seems to be a simplified version of the model 1910 with an eight-button front and buttoned Swedish cuffs. Probably carried over from the Reichwehr period it is field grey and shows the rank of Schutze (private). Obscured by his arms are two slanted pockets with flaps. He wears the oval machine-embroidered Gebirgsjäger Edelweiss patch on his right upper arm and on the other arm his Nachrichten (signals) speciality/trade patch which is a red lightning bolt on a black woollen backing. His breast eagle appears to be white on a dark green or black backing.

This Gebirgsjäger Feldwebel is also wearing his Service Visor cap with metal Edelweiss insignia. The crown wire stiffener has been removed to give it the popular 'veteran' appearance. His tunic is the 1936 pattern with a dark green collar and NCO Tresse and his shoulder straps have the numerals '85' in pressed white metal just above his rank pip. The 85th Gebirgs-Infanterie Regiment was part of the 5th Gebirgs Division commanded by General Ringel and took part in Operation Merkur (Mercury) the invasion of Crete, in May 1941. His ribbon bar contains the Iron Cross 2nd Class, and an army service medal, the remainder unknown. Below that, his War Merit Cross 1st Class with Swords, his Infantry Assault badge and Winter Campaign in the East medal.

This young Gebirgsjäger is wearing his model 1943 Service Field tunic with a flat-woven grey thread eagle on a field grey backing. His Iron Cross 2nd Class ribbon is in his buttonhole and he has a wound badge on his left breast pocket. Besides his new bride, he holds his Bergmütze (mountain cap) which was similar to the 1943 Einheitsfeldmütze but with a shorter peak. The design was taken from the Austrian army Service cap. It carries the two-part pressed metal Edelweiss badge on the left side. Just visible in his right breast pocket is a whistle and lanyard.

This somewhat older Gebirgsjäger is also wearing his 1943 Service Field tunic with the same style breast eagle as previously seen. His Edelweiss arm patch, however is far more detailed than the usual machine-embroidered type and is therefore, probably a privately-purchased item. In his tunic buttonhole are his Iron Cross 2nd Class and Winter Campaign in the East ribbons.

■ This Leutnant's (second-lieutenant) Officers' Service Visor cap has embroidered National Eagle insignia and wreathed cockade with silver bullion cap cords. His pre-war Tuchrock (Service tunic) was quite probably worn throughout the war and it carries his rank collar patches. His shoulder boards of silver bullion, without a single gilt metal star on each, indicates his rank of junior lieutenant. The silver embroidered breast eagle seems to be the later pattern with a raised tail. On his left breast are the Iron Cross 1st and 2nd Class, what appears to be the Deutsches Schutzwall-Ehrenzeichen (West Wall medal), the Erdkampfabzeichen der Luftwaffe (Ground Combat badge, the Flakkampfabzeichen (anti-aircraft badge) and a Verwundetenabzeichen (wound badge) in black. Hanging on his left side is the second pattern Offizierdolch (Officers' dagger) with regulation portepee.

This dashing Leutnant also sports a Service Visor cap with silver bullion embroidered insignia. The shoulder boards and collar patches have a very light backing colour (yellow?) which indicates his service as aircrew. Unfortunately the two medal ribbons on his left breast are unclear.

■ Here is another view of the same happy couple. He wears a floral sprig on his left lapel and on his left breast is his observers' badge which was instituted in 1936. Just below that is his DRL sports badge. In his left hand he holds his Officers' dagger with portepee.

This Oberst (colonel), photographed with his wife and grandchildren is wearing a plethora of medal ribbons, among them: the 1914-1918 Iron Cross, Reich War Service Cross, 1914-1918 Cross of Honour with Swords, Bavarian Military Service Cross and the Luftwaffe Armed Forces Long Service medal. On his left breast pocket are the 1939-1945 Iron Cross 1st Class and below that the Knight's Cross of the War Merit Cross with Swords 1st Class. His shoulder boards are plaited silver bullion braid with two stars.

This Luftwaffe Feldwebel (sergeant) is wearing his ORs' Service Visor cap with white summer top and pressed white metal National Eagle and Wreathed Cockade with wings. His Tuchrock carries the early style machine-embroidered eagle with a droop tail on his right breast pocket. On his left breast he wears his Wehrmacht Service medal and below that a radio operator/air gunner badge.

This very youthful Obergefreiter (leading aircraftman) is wearing his regulation ORs' Service Visor cap with pressed white metal insignia. His Fliegerbluse (Flight Blouse) is the post-1940 version with side pockets and on his left sleeve he wears the appropriate rank chevrons. On his left breast we see a ribbon for the War Merit Cross with Swords and his "God-fearing" floral sprig.

A Feldwebel with white-topped ORs' Service Visor cap. His Fliegerbluse carries several decorations: in his button hole, the Winter Campaign in the East medal, next to that his Iron Cross 2nd Class and below the Erdkampfabzeichen (ground combat) and Flakkampfabzeichen (flak gunners' badge). Below that, his DRL sports badge and on his left arm his machine-woven anti-aircraft artillery speciality/trade patch.

This Obergefreiter (leading aircraftman) is wearing an ORs' Service Visor cap with dark Waffenfarbe (arm of service piping). On his 1940-style Fliegerbluse he has a lanyard with whistle attached and rank chevrons on his sleeve. Below that is his speciality/trade patch denoting technical personnel.

A young Feldwebel pilot with ORs' Service Visor cap, again with pressed metal insignia is wearing a marksman's lanyard and probably a pilot/observer and a DRL sports badge. His tunic is the post-1940 version of the Fliegerbluse and at his left side hangs his Officers' dagger the wearing of which, with portepee, was extended to all NCOs after March 1940.

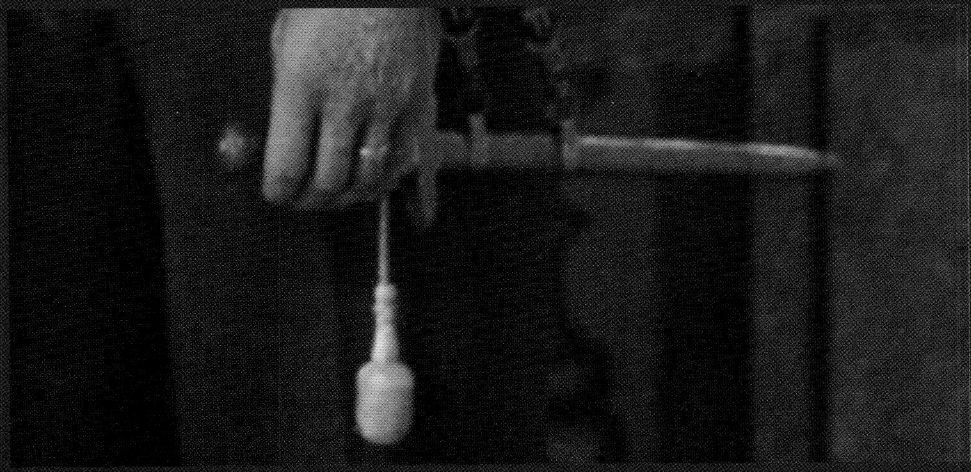

With Wehrmacht wedding guests behind him, this Luftwaffe Feldwebel is wearing the regulation Service Visor cap and the earlier Tuchrock with Oberfähnrich (advanced officer candidate) stripes on his cuffs. His breast eagle is the early droop-tail type and he appears to have service medals on his left breast with the DRL sports badge below. On his left side he wears the Fliegerschwert (flyers' sword).

A good view is afforded of the ORs' Service Visor cap with its metal insignia. This Feldwebel wears the later pattern breast eagle and has the Iron Cross 2nd Class ribbon in his buttonhole. On his left breast pocket of his Tuchrock is his DRL sports badge, while on his left sleeve his speciality/trade badge is just visible, denoting him as a Schirrmeister (motor transport/storeman). Clasped in his left hand is his Officers' dagger with portepee.

This Luftwaffe Feldwebel's Service Visor cap clearly shows a dark Waffenfarbe, matching his collar patches. His 2nd model 1940 Fliegerbluse (with pockets) is adorned with marksman's lanyard, a machine-woven breast eagle and religious sprig. On his left side he wears DRL and SA sports badges and his Officers' dagger and portepee.

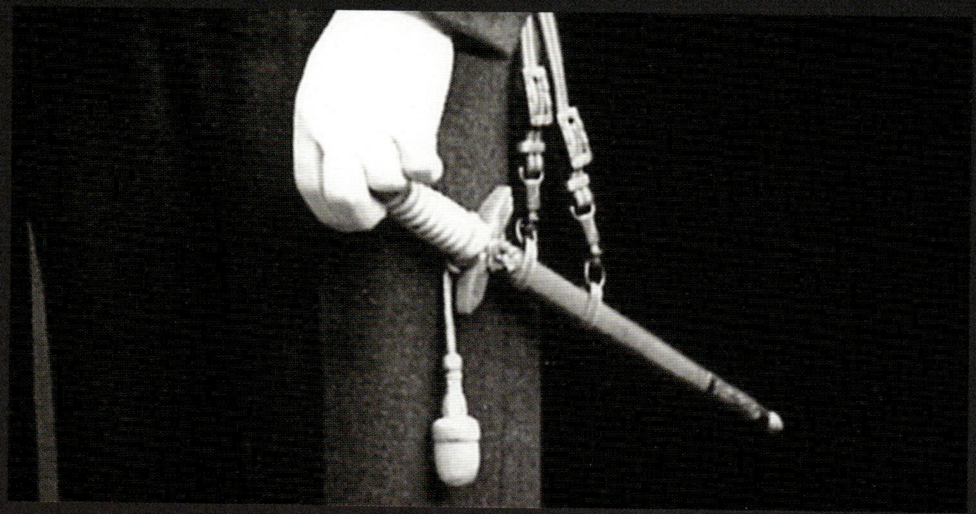

A nice photograph of an Obergefreiter, wearing the ORs' Service Visor cap with metal insignia and the Fliegerbluse with rank stripes on his left sleeve.

A fun photograph of a couple wearing the uniform of a Luftwaffe Gefreiter. It's hard to tell who might wear the trousers in that household! She is wearing the ORs' Fliegermütze (Flight cap) and has a teletype operators' speciality/trade badge on her left sleeve with ORs' belt and aluminium buckle and high marching boots. Her 'friend', apart from the carpet slippers, is wearing the ORs' Service Visor cap and ORs' greatcoat with Gefreiters' rank collar patches and sleeve chevron. This happy and obviously loyal couple (perhaps father and daughter) pose beneath a portrait of their Führer.

This Feldwebel has pinched in his pressed aluminium National Eagle insignia on his Service cap to create a more worn, crushed effect to suggest that he is an 'old hand'. The shoulder straps on his post-1940 Fliegerbluse carry the rank stripe of an Unteroffizieranwärter (NCO candidate) and below his religious sprig we see his Hitler Youth Proficiency Award and DRL sports badge. Around his waist is the ORs' belt and buckle and on his left sleeve, rank chevrons and a speciality/trade badge for a Geprüfter Fernsprecher (qualified telephone operator).

A charming photograph, but also a nice clear one showing the ORs' Service Visor cap with pressed metal Nation Eagle and winged wreathed cockade, also the ribbed material that makes up the cap band. His Feldbluse has Obegefreiter rank collar patches with what appears to be silver/aluminium bullion piping around the actual collar (usually an indication of Oberfähnrich (officer candidate), but his shoulder straps carry the silver Tresse (edging) identifying him as an Unteroffizieranwärter (NCO candidate).

This young man is a member of the Herman Göring Panzer Regiment. His Service Visor cap would seem to be a white-piped, ex-Allegemeine (general) SS cap with bullion embroidered Luftwaffe eagle insignia whilst retaining the early pressed metal SS 'jawless' skull. His black panzer wrap-over tunic is also somewhat unusual in that he has rather overt piping around the large collar and his HG white-backed collar patches have the pressed metal panzer skull positioned at the base of the patches rather than, as is more usual, in the middle. His decorations are the Iron Cross 2nd Class, the wound badge and the DRL sports badge. He has a standard ORs' belt with white metal buckle and on his left arm are his rank chevrons and speciality/trade badge of the Kraftfahrer (motor vehicle driver). His bride is wearing the traditional black wedding gown, worn in parts of pre-1945 Germany.

Another Luftwaffe NCO. His Fliegerbluse carries what appear to be white-piped collar patches with the rank of Obergefreiter. His breast eagle is the later style with raised tail and is machine woven. On his left sleeve are his rank chevrons.

This Feldwebel pilot is wearing his pre-1940 Fliegerbluse (without pockets) on which is pinned his "God-fearing" status religious sprig of flowers. On his left breast is what appears to be a Prague Castle award with bar and below that his pilots' or pilot/observer badge. His ORs' Service cap has dark Waffenfarbe (piping).

This Luftwaffe Unteroffizier is wearing his Tuchrock with a machine-woven ORs' breast eagle. Apart from his sprig of flowers he has the Fliegertechnisches Personal (flying technical personnel) embroidered speciality/trade patch on his left cuff. Below that is what appears to be a mourning band of some sort. His ORs' Service cap carries the regulation pressed white metal insignia and hanging from his left side is his bayonet with Faustriemen (knot).

Here is another NCO from the Fliegertechnisches Personal. His rank collar shows that he is a Feldwebel and his Fliegerbluse left breast displays his War Service Cross with Swords and the Italy/Africa medal. On his head he wears the Model 43 Einheitsfeldmütze (Visored Field cap) with single button flap and machine-woven National Eagle and cockade insignia.

This Luftwaffe Obergefreiter is wearing (apart from his rather unusual nightcap) a regulation Luftwaffe Tropical Field Service uniform. The breast eagle is machine-woven but unusually the backing material is a dark colour rather than tan. The Uberfallhose (overtrousers) are the style much-favoured by the Fallschirmtruppe (paratroops) and are easily identified by the large map pocket on the left thigh (see next page).

Here is another photograph of the same bride and groom. We can clearly see the map pocket on his left thigh and his Obergefreiter rank chevrons on his left arm. He too wears a religious floral sprig on his lapel. His boots are non-typical in that they are only part lace- hole, part stud and are possibly a private purchase.

A Luftwaffe Unteroffizier with his family. He wears regulation insignia on his Fliegerbluse. His breast eagle is machine-woven on a blue-grey backing.

Another Luftwaffe NCO with his family. He holds the rank of Obergefreiter and is also wearing the Fliegerbluse. In his button hole are the ribbons of the Iron Cross 2nd Class and the Winterschlact Im Osten Medal (Winter Campaign in the East) which was also known by the troops as the 'frozen meat award'. Apart from his rank chevrons on his arm, he also is wearing the ground combat badge of the Luftwaffe, the Luftwaffe flak badge and a wound badge.

This Feldwebel is wearing a relatively unadorned Fliegerbluse. Apart from his regulation shoulder straps and collar patches, on his left arm is a qualified teletype operators' speciality/trade badge.

A fairly typical example of a page from a serviceman's photographic album. This Obergefreiter pilot is wearing his Tuchrock (four-pocket Service tunic). On his left breast pocket flap we see the glider instructors' enamel badge and just below that either the pilots' or pilot/observer badge.

This Feldwebel is also wearing a glider instructors' badge on his Tuchrock, but one that appears to be embroidered in silver bullion.

A very smart couple pictured here. The groom is wearing his Tuchrock with rank insignia for an Unteroffizier. His breast eagle of machine-woven white thread is the later post-1939 style. His medal ribbon above his left breast pocket flap appears to be a Luftwaffe service award and below that is his DRL sports badge. On his left hip we can just see his model 1884/98 bayonet with knot.

This Luftwaffe Obegefreiter is wearing a pre-1940 Fliegerbluse (without pockets) and has a motor vehicle drivers' speciality/trade patch on his left sleeve. Below his religious floral sprig is what could be a Blood Order ribbon. Below that is his SA sports badge. Hanging from his ORs' belt, with pressed white metal buckle, is his bayonet.

The Fliegerbluse is shown being worn by this Obegefreiter with a wound badge in black on his left breast. His whistle lanyard hangs from his left lapel and just visible is his bayonet, which appears to be nickel-plated. The happy bride wears the traditional black wedding dress with a white veil signifying her 'maiden' status. This style of dress went out of fashion after 1945.

An Unteroffizier is pictured here wearing the post-1940 Fliegerbluse. Below his floral sprig hangs a small crucifix and below that, his pilots' or pilot/observer badge. Below that we see a glider instructors' embroidered bullion badge and a DRL sports badge. A chained flyers' dagger hangs from his ORs' belt.

Another Obergefreiter in his Fliegerbluse. This young man wears his whistle and lanyard and has the motor vehicle drivers' speciality/trade badge on his sleeve. The award on his left breast is probably the DRL sports badge.

This Unteroffizier is wearing his pre-1940 style Fliegerbluse, on which hangs a marksmans' lanyard. On his left sleeve we see a machine-embroidered anti-aircraft artillery speciality/trade Badge. Note the black leather Marschstiefel (marching boots). His NCO's Service Visor cap has its wire stiffener in place inside the crown and the insignia is the usual pressed white metal eagle and winged cockade.

Another example of the Fliegerbluse, but this time a post-1940 version with pockets. His ORs' Service Visor cap with pressed white metal insignia has been given the 'crushed' look, so often favoured by servicemen by removing the wire crown stiffener.

Portraying the perfect German family, this rather more mature NCO is wearing his Service tunic with regulation Feldwebel insignia. Unfortunately his medal ribbon and badge on his left breast are unclear.

This wedding couple have arrived for the ceremony in a rather grand manner, in a horse-drawn carriage. What is unusual is that the driver is a Waffen-SS enlisted man of the LAH (Leibstandarte Adolf Hitler) Division as can be seen from the LAH monogram on his shoulder straps. The groom is also an enlisted man and is wearing his NCOs' Service Visor cap. Just visible on his left breast is his pilots' badge.

The same couple are shown seated in front of the NSDAP functionaries who are to perform the marriage ceremony. On either side are the runic candleholders that signify life.

Standing to make their vows, the groom reveals his chained flyers' dagger hanging from his left side. Also, just above his left breast pocket flap button is what appears to be an NSDAP badge, which would account for the heavy political presence at the ceremony.

As the Luftwaffe pilot NCO places the wedding ring on his bride's finger, he is flanked by an NSDAP officer and a young Bund Deutscher Mädel (League of German Girls).

Signing the registry. As the groom signs he affords us a good view of his flyers' dagger and chain hanger and a good profile of his ORs' Service Visor cap.

The father of this happy family group is wearing a regulation ORs' Flight cap with machine woven white thread insignia. His collar patches and sleeve rank chevrons on his post-1940 Fiegerbluse reveal him to be an Obergefreiter. His bayonet can be seen hanging from his ORs' belt and buckle. On his feet are the black leather marching boots.

This couple are both in the service of the Reich. She is a Wehrmacht auxiliary, possibly in signals (note the lightning bolt enamel badge on her tie). He wears a Flight cap and Fliegerbluse with Gefreiter collar patches and sleeve rank chevron. He has a bayonet hanging from his ORs' belt and buckle.

This Luftwaffe Flieger, or more probably Kanonier (from his red artillery collar patches) is wearing the ORs' Service Visor cap and the post-1940 Fliegerbluse.

This Luftwaffe Unteroffizier is wearing a post-1940 Fliegerbluse (with pockets) and ORs' Service Visor cap with pressed white metal insignia. From his belt hangs his model 84/98 bayonet in its leather frog and Tröddel (knot).

This young Fallschirmjäger (paratrooper) is wearing his jump helmet (model 1938 stahlhelm) and his early-style 2nd pattern Fallschirmschützenbluse (jump smock). The 2nd pattern being a step-in design, the early version of which was without pockets and the colour was a plain grey-green. Later patterns opened out completely for ease of entry, had zip pockets and splinter pattern camouflage printing. He wears the regulation breast eagle which was machine woven. His brown leather gloves are specially designed for paratroops with long elasticated cuffs. Later patterns were shorter. His belt and buckle are the standard Luftwaffe ORs' type and the olive green knee protectors are again the early type (without camouflage printing). His boots, however, are the later pattern which lace up at the front and have leather soles rather than the early side-lacing type, with rubber soles.

This Fallschirmjäger Unteroffizier is wearing his Tuchrock with white thread machine-woven breast eagle and unusually the floral sprig just below that. On his left breast are: the Iron Cross 2nd Class, Spanish Campaign medal and Red Military Service Cross, all won in service with Legion Condor in Spain. Below that we just see his Fallschirmschützen Abzeichen (parachutists' qualification badge).

This Fallschirmjäger Unteroffizier also wears his Tuchrock. Below his floral sprig is his Iron Cross 1st Class, below that on the left his ground combat badge and his parachutists' qualification badge on the right. Below all of these he has a wound badge in black. On his left sleeve is the NCO armourers' speciality/trade badge and below that, his Crete armband signifying him to be a veteran of Operation Mercury, the airborne assault on the island in May 1941.

The first in a series of photographs depicting a 'proxy' marriage, which is one that takes place simultaneously at the front and at home. This particular one is actually taking place in the field with a table adorned with a swastika flag and large photograph of the head of the Luftwaffe, Hermann Göring. Obscured by the guard is also a large framed photograph of Adolf Hitler. This young Fallschirmjäger Leutnant is flanked by a guard of honour in a camouflaged helmet and jump smock on the left and by a 75mm Panzerabwehrkanone (anti-tank gun) on the right.

The second image in this series shows the groom saluting a fellow officer in a model 43 Einheitsfeldmütze (Peaked Field cap) who is carrying a Walther PPK or PP pistol and holster on his belt. The groom is wearing his post-1940 Fliegerbluse and fallschirm trousers with snap-closure pockets. Around his waist is the regulation Officers' double claw buckle and brown leather belt.

The Leutnant (second lieutenant) has the wedding ring placed on his finger by his commanding officer who is an Oberleutnant (lieutenant). This officer is wearing the Luftwaffe Bergmütze (Peaked Field cap) with a single button flap. It is the ORs' version, apparently without Officers' bullion piping around the crown, but he does have a pinched white metal eagle rather than the more usual machine-woven cap insignia. The groom wears his Schirmmütze (Service Visor cap) with silver bullion or aluminium embroidered National Eagle and cockade. His Officers' cap cords are also of twisted, woven aluminium braid, as opposed to the ORs' pattern which has a leather-type chinstrap. On his shoulder boards we can just make out the letter 'P' which signifies him to be from a panzerjäger (anti-tank unit).

After the ceremony the newlywed Officer is joined by two NCOs. The Feldwebel on the left has an embroidered parachutist's qualification badge on his left breast, while his comrade opposite is a Oberfeldwebel (sergeant-major), both are wearing the post-1940 Fliegerbluse. The groom has the Iron Cross 2nd class ribbon on his Fliegerbluse, below that his Iron Cross 1st Class and a wound badge in black.

His Service Visor cap has had the wire stiffener removed which gives the hat a much more used feel which in turn would make it clear to all that he is a soldier of no-little experience. His comrades hold a photograph of the bride set in a plastic and metal frame, surrounded with roses. A good view of the Officers' belt is afforded here.

A rather grand wedding ceremony with high-ranking SS and SA officers and party functionaries attending.

The caption reads: "Wedding of the director of the Nationalsozialistische Volkswohlfahrt [NSV] Ostmark. Today in registry office IX in Vienna, the director of the NSV in the east, SS-Standartenführer [colonel] and Reichsstellenleiter Wilhelm Janowsky to Miss Eleonore Slasszstatt. At 13.00 hours in the ceremony hall of the Ehefeier town castle they are listening to the speech given by Pg. Walter Habenbrock, Reichsschuldungsbeauftragter."

The NSV (National Socialist People's Welfare) was responsible for citizens' welfare and charitable work. Seated behind the bride is another SS officer, SS-Gruppenführer (major-general), Seyss-Inquart. He was instrumental in the successful annexation of Austria in 1937 and became its Reichstatthalter (governor). Later, in 1940, he was appointed Reichs Commissioner for the Netherlands and was arrested at the end of the war, tried at Nuremberg and subsequently hanged. He is wearing the black Officers' version of the Service tunic with silver bullion piping around the collar. His right sleeve carries the 'old fighters' chevron, denoting his early activity in the NSDAP and silver bullion aiguillettes hang from his right shoulder board. On his black tie is his enamel party badge and just visible is his SS Officers' honour sword on his left side.

The groom has elected to wear his Gesellschaftsanzug (formal evening dress uniform) with silver bullion aiguillettes under which can be seen his Totenkopf (deaths' head) breast badge. The collar and cuffs are piped in silver. We see his single silver bullion oak leaf spray SS-Standartenführer rank collar patch and his Allegemeine-SS brassard with black borders on his left sleeve. His General Officers' Service Visor cap is piped in silver with silver bullion cap cords with the eagle and Totenkopf insignia probably in silver, or silver-plated. Note that the trousers to the formal evening uniform have silver Tresse bordered with white piping down the outside seams. Under his jacket is a white waistcoat and shirt with stand-up collar and white bow tie.

Here we see an SS-Untersturmführer (2nd lieutenent) and his bride on their wedding day, flanked by an air force NCO with summer white-topped Service Visor cap and a marksmanship lanyard. The older gentleman on the other side is wearing the Reichsluftschutzbund (air defence organisation) Mützenadler (cap eagle). On his left breast he has the Treudienst Ehrenzeichen (faithful service award) and SA sports badge. The groom wears his Officers' Service Visor cap with pressed white metal SS-style eagle and Totenkopf (death's head) insignia with silver bullion cap cords. He is also wearing Officers' aiguillettes as per regulations for official or other public functions. On his left breast he has the Deutshcher Reichsbund fur Leibesubungen (DRL) and Sturmabteilung (SA) sports badges and has an Officers' SS brocade belt with white metal clasp around his waist. His SS Officers' sword hangs from his left side and as with all SS ranks in field grey uniform, the SS eagle is on his left sleeve, the Officers' version being embroidered in silver bullion. His tunic is the 1936 pattern and his riding breeches are tucked into his spurred riding boots.

This romantic couple are pictured somewhere in the snow. The Waffen-SS Officer is wearing his Service Visor cap with silver bullion cap cords and coloured Waffenfarbe (arm of service piping). He wears a sheepskin-lined greatcoat with a large collar, which despite his officer rank sports an ORs' machine-woven arm eagle on the sleeve. His shoulder boards carry a single pip and are for an SS-Obersturmführer (lieutenant). Just above the pip there is a barely visible unidentified pressed-metal insignia, possibly a Sanitatsdienst (medical service) snake and rod symbol.

This Waffen-SS NCO has the collar patch rank of SS-Rottenführer (corporal). His tunic is the 1936 type, easily recognisable by the dark green collar. Above his left breast pocket is the Anschluss ribbon for taking part in the annexation of Austria. The hat he wears is the 1938 soft-Visored Field cap for ORs with the peak covered in the same material as the crown. The insignia of eagle and death's head is of pressed white metal. His partner wears the Hitler Jugend enamel diamond-shaped badge on her left lapel and another unidentified badge, possibly an SS supporter's pin.

A Waffen-SS Oberscharführer (staff sergeant) and bride on their wedding day. He too is wearing the 1936 pattern tunic with dark green collar and NCO Tresse in silver around the edges. There is an unidentified emblem on his shoulder board between the pip and the button, which could be a company number within his unit. His cap is probably a 1938 style 'crusher' or 'semi-crusher' in that the peak is of soft leather and the cap itself has no chinstrap. With the wire stiffening in the crown removed, it allowed it to be handled roughly during use or crushed flat for storage. He has medals on his left breast, however only the War Merit Cross with Swords in bronze is visible.

This young couple are pictured here atop a British-produced Triumph motorcycle. His rank is SS-Rottenführer and his collar patches on his 1936 tunic are the early type, having a black and white twisted cord edge. This cord was discontinued after 1940. His embroidered large LAH shoulder straps and Adolf Hitler cufftitle, identify him as being a member of the Leibstandarte SS Adolf Hitler, the premier Waffen-SS formation. Immediately below his arm eagle are his SS-Rottenführer rank chevrons. He wears issue motorcycle goggles over his old style Field cap with a triangular, machine-woven eagle insignia on the left side. Lastly, he wears long leather marching boots.

The same couple, seen here on a bench. Here we can just see his medal ribbons, which look to be for the Czechoslovakian and Austrian annexations.

This family photograph shows an SS-Unterscharführer (corporal) wearing a 1940 pattern tunic with field grey painted domed metal buttons and NCO Tresse around the collar patches and shoulder straps. His SS runic collar patch is machine-embroidered in silver-grey thread. On his left breast is a medal ribbon bar, possibly the Iron Cross. It is hard to say, with any confidence without any sign of combat awards or cufftitle, that he is a member of the Waffen-SS as this configuration of field grey tunic and rank insignia was worn by many branches of the burgeoning SS organisation.

This SS NCO is wearing his pre-war black Service Dress uniform. His right collar patch has an unidentified Standarte number embroidered on it, while his left collar patch displays his rank of SS-Sturmann. Notice the early twisted black and white cord edging, also on his shoulder straps. He has the NSDAP badge pinned onto his issue black tie. His Service cap is the black ORs' Visor type with white metal insignia and leather chinstraps.

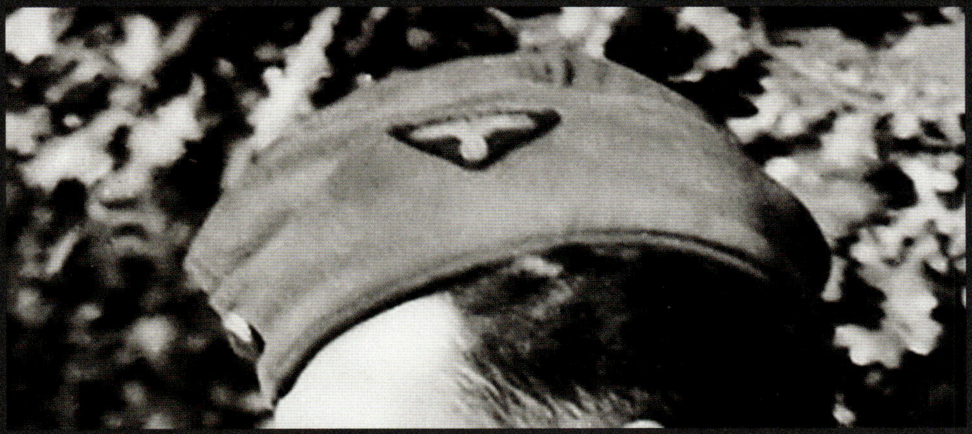

■ This SS-Rottenführer is wearing his old model Field cap with triangular eagle insignia patch sewn onto the left side. On the front of the cap we see the button with its death's head motif in relief. His greatcoat carries the smaller and therefore later style LAH monogram shoulder straps, his ORs' machine embroidered sleeve eagle, rank chevrons and Adolf Hitler cuff title. Around his waist we see his regulation ORs' leather belt with pressed white metal buckle, hanging from which is his model 84/98 bayonet and leather frog.

This SS soldier is a Hauptscharführer (sergeant-major). His tunic, although the older 1936 pattern, has more up-to-date collar patches with silver NCOs' Tresse dating from 1940 onwards. He has the Iron Cross 2nd Class in his button hole, an army service medal ribbon and what might be a Spanish civil war Honour Cross. Below these is his DRL sports badge. His arm eagle is the ORs' machine-woven type on black backing cloth. He has what is probably a privately-purchased ORs' Service Visor cap which seems to be white-piped (infantry), but all arms of service colour piping were changed to white in November 1940 and so it is possible that he might not be infantry at all. A good view of the pressed white metal 1936 pattern SS eagle and 1934 pattern full-jawed death's head is afforded, as is the patent-leather chinstrap with its twin sliding buckles.

The groom is a member of the 4th SS Polizei Division. He is of Rottenführer rank according to his post-1940 collar patch. The tunic is a model 1940, interestingly without pleated pockets and the left sleeve carries his machine-woven eagle and rank chevron. Below those he wears his SS Polizei Division cuff title. His medal ribbons are the World War I Iron Cross 1st Class and the Winter Campaign in the East. His belt is the standard ORs' type and his cap appears to be the ORs' Service Visor pattern with the chinstraps removed. This was often done in order to give the cap a crusher-type style. Note that the pressed-metal eagle cap badge above the death's dead is not the SS type but that of the army.

Here we have a good view of the 1940 pattern tunic, being worn in the open-collar mode. This Waffen-SS NCO carries the rank collar patch of SS-Sturmann (private). On his left sleeve is a flat-woven arm eagle. Below that is his rank chevron and diamond-shaped speciality/trade patch for signals. At the bottom of his sleeve is a clear view of his OR's Der Führer regiment cufftitle in machine-woven silver-grey thread and silver bullion edging. The Der Führer Regiment was one of the regiments comprising the 2nd SS Panzer Division Das Reich. On his left breast pocket is a wound badge, which could be in black with the paint having worn off through wear, or a higher silver or gold classification. His OR's belt has the white pressed metal buckle and he has the Iron Cross 2nd Class and Winter Campaign in the east medal ribbons in his buttonhole. Lastly, his ORs' Service Visor cap carries the regulation pressed white metal insignia, the eagle of which has been pinched to create a more flamboyant shape to the crown of the cap.

This SS-Rottenführer is wearing his ORs' black Service Visor cap with pressed white metal insignia, patent leather chinstrap and regulation white piping around the crown and cap band. The wire stiffener is still in place around the crown, giving it a smooth, curved shape. His tunic is the 1932 pattern black Service type with twisted black and white cord edging around the collar and collar patches. He also wears a brown SA shirt suggesting that this photograph was taken before mid-1936 when white shirts replaced the brown. His trousers are the piped, Full-Dress pattern. On his tie is a NSDAP enamel badge and on his left breast the SA sports badge. The 1925 version of the SS Kampfbinde (brassard) is on his left sleeve, later to be replaced in 1938, when SS uniforms changed to field grey, by an embroidered SS eagle. Over his tunic is a black leather cross strap and belt with a white metal ORs' buckle. His cuff title denotes that he is a member of a 1st Sturm, Fuss-Standarte.

This Leibstandarte Hauptscharführer (sergeant-major) of the Führerbegleit-kommando (Hitler's personal guard unit) is wearing full dress uniform for his wedding. His shoulder straps and collar patches have the black and white twisted cord edging and on his breast pocket is his DRL sports badge and 1931 Brunswick Rally SA commemorative badge. On his left arm he wears the regulation SS brassard and below that the Adolf Hitler inscribed cuff title in silver bullion thread. A gold NSDAP membership badge is worn on his tie and an Officers' Dress sword and portepee hangs from his left side. His NCOs' Service Visor cap retains its crown stiffener. Behind him is his commanding officer, SS-Sturmbannführer (major) Bruno Gesche, head of the Führerbegleit-kommando. His Officers' Service Visor cap has bullion cap cords and quite possibly silver-plated insignia. The cap band is black velvet rather than the woollen ORs' version. Aiguillettes are worn on his tunic, also an NSDAP badge and Officers' sword with portepee on his hip.

This rather serious SS man wears a 1936 pattern tunic with post-1940 NCO Tresse around the collar. His rank collar patch indicates SS-Oberscharführer (sergeant), as does the single pip on his shoulder strap. We see a flat-woven arm eagle on his left sleeve and a silver or gold wound badge and what looks like a DRL sports badge on his left breast pocket. A medal ribbon bar sits above his floral sprig but is unclear. His ORs' Service Visor cap is held under his arm, gloves and long straight-leg trousers with shoes complete the uniform.

This early group photograph includes eight members of the SS (one of which, being the groom). Their Service Visor caps are a mixture of styles, with and without crown stiffeners. At least four carry the early 'jawless' skull, but the groom has the later 'full jaw' 1934 version. All have the early style cap eagle. Most of them wear the black belt and cross strap and twisted black and white corded collar patch edging. Their Standarte-numbered right collar patches are unclear. The groom's shoulder straps are the 1934 pattern with black and white twisted cord on a black wool backing. One of the SS guests is an Officer with silver bullion cap cords and an Untersturmführers' (1st lieutenants') three-pip rank collar patch. It is interesting that the groom wears a religious floral sprig on his left lapel, which is unusual for SS men who were expected to be without religious ties, loyal only to Adolf Hitler. Brown shirts are being worn by all the SS men, suggesting that the date of the photograph is pre-1936. The SS man at far left wears riding breeches and boots, while the groom wears straight trousers and shoes. At the rear can be seen another guest wearing an SA Service Visor cap with silver bullion cords indicating officer status. Beside the SS Officer stands a man wearing an unidentified SA-style kepi of dark colour, possibly NSKK (motor corps).

A rare photograph of an SS-Fallschirmjäger (paratrooper). His rank of SS-Mann (private) is shown by his blank black left collar patch. His tunic is the 1944 Service type. His Iron Cross 1st Class hangs from an SS enamel lapel pin and on his breast pocket flap is the Finnish commemorative award for operations on the northern front. Below those are his wound badge in black and Fallschirmjäger qualification badge. His ORs' belt buckle appears to be nickel-plated and his flat machine-woven SS arm eagle is just visible above his extremely rare ORs' machine embroidered SS-Fallschirmjäger cuff title.

This early photograph of an Allegemeine-SS trooper shows him wearing his ORs' Service Visor cap with wire stiffener in place. It carries the early political 1936-style broad-winged NSDAP eagle rather than the more usual pointed thin-winged type. His shirt is brown and his collar and shoulder strap are also early types. The collar patches are without insignia giving no indication of rank other than by his cap style. His SS brassard is just visible on his left arm. Indeed, an idyllic SS family scene with wife, children, cat and chicken.

This young man is an SS-Gebirgsjäger (mountain trooper). His oval machine-embroidered SS Edelweiss patch is carried on the right upper arm of his 1943 Service tunic. His rank collar patch and shoulder straps with Tresse signify that he is an Unterscharführer (sergeant). In his buttonhole is the ribbon for the Winter Campaign in the East medal.

This junior sergeant of the Ordnungspolizei (order police) is wearing his Service tunic with brown collar and matching brown-buttoned cuffs. He carries the Polizei machine-embroidered badge on his upper left arm (an eagle across an oval wreath). His Service Visor cap retains its' wire crown stiffener and his police eagle insignia in pressed white metal is worn on the cap band below the cockade. His police sword and portepee are suspended from a hanger, although it is not clear if he is wearing a belt.

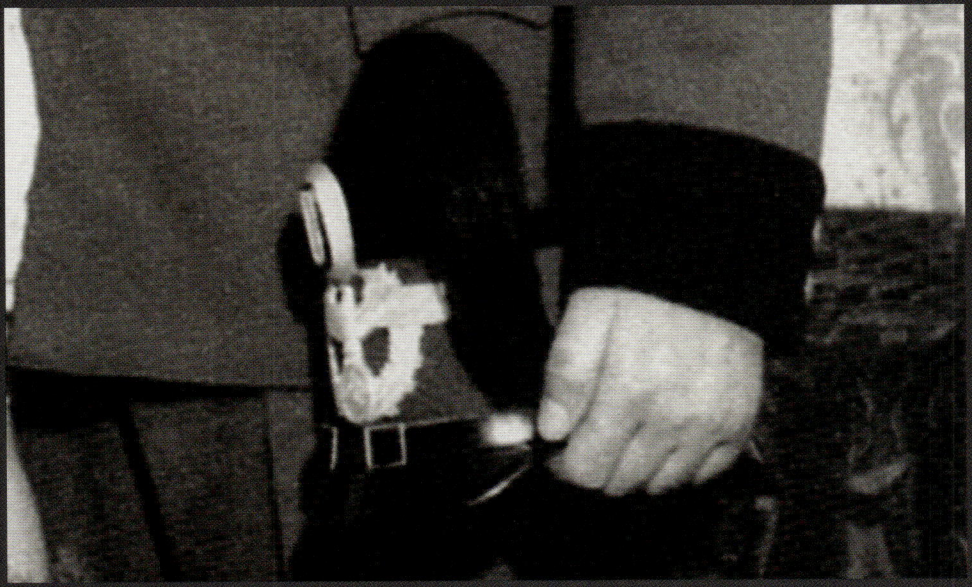

This mature groom is wearing his Ordnungspolizei Service uniform with white patent leather parade ORs' belt, buckle and wide cross-strap. Below his left breast pocket is his Deutshcher Reichsbund fur Leibesubungen (DRL) and SA sports badges. His rank shoulder straps indicate that he is a Hauptwachtmeister (senior sergeant) and he is holding his Tschako (shako) with black horsehair plume. ORs' caps carried a leather chinstrap or white metal chin scales for parade duty. The large police eagle and wreath insignia is in pressed white metal.

This Ordnungspolizei Wachtmeister (sergeant) is wearing his shako with black plume and black,white and red oval cockade above the cap eagle and wreath. He has a floral sprig pinned to his tunic and is wearing a white patent leather parade belt and cross-strap, from which hangs his parade bayonet and Tröddel (side arm tassel for ORs).

Here we see an Oberwachtmeister (sergeant) of the Ordnungspolizei with his bride. His Service Visor cap has had the stiffener removed and is being worn at a somewhat jaunty angle. He has a floral sprig indicating that he is 'God-fearing' and has an SA sports badge on his left breast. At his left side can be seen his parade sword.

This rather romantically posed photograph shows another Ordungspolizei of Wachtmeister rank with his regulation Service Visor cap and his police badge on his arm. He has several medal ribbons on the bar above his left breast, but they are too indistinct to identify with any certainty. Below those are his DRL and SA sports badges and his dress sword.

The tunic that this Hitler Jugend leader is wearing is very similar to the Service tunic worn by the NSDAP leadership, but with the lower, larger button-down pockets having scalloped flaps and two shoulder boards which carry his rank. On his upper left arm is his triangular regional unit patch, below that his HJ brassard and below that, his motor sports school badge. His left breast pocket has his small enamel HJ marksmanship badge and his Goldenes Ehrenzeichen der Hitlerjugend mit Eichenlaubkranz (enamel golden HJ honour badge with oak leaves). Below that, is the DRL sports badge. Black breeches are tucked into high-quality riding boots.

This Hitler Jugend leader, possibly an Oberbannführer (senior banner leader), is wearing his black four-pocket Service tunic with pleated breast pockets. A whistle lanyard hangs from his left shoulder strap. He appears to have the golden honour badge with oak leaves on his left breast pocket. His belt and cross-strap is the Officers' style with double clawed buckle. An HJ brassard is worn on his left sleeve. Just below his left elbow we can see his Fahrtenmesser (HJ knife) scabbard hanging from his belt. The Service Visor cap carries the political 1936-style National Eagle and below that the HJ enamel diamond insignia. The cap has light piping around the crown and a leather chinstrap. The cap band appears to be a different, lighter colour from the black crown.

This man is an NSDAP Stellenleiter (office head) at one of the Gau (regional) offices. The collars have a system of bullion Tresse to signify rank. He wears the Ausgeheanzug (walking-out dress uniform).

This rather dramatic photograph shows an NSDAP Hauptstellenleiter (senior office head) wearing his Dienstanzug (service/office tunic). His 1937 pattern NSDAP political leaders' Visor cap carries the 1939 political eagle insignia and wreath with cockade, with the centre of the cockade carrying a small swastika. The insignia are in a pressed gilt-coloured metal and the officers'-style cap cords are in gold bullion. The ribbon bar on his left breast pocket has the World War I Iron Cross, the War Merit Cross with Swords and the NSDAP Long Service medal.

■ Another NSDAP Hauptstellenleiter. His Service Visor cap has the same insignia as shown previously but the cap itself has a much more rounded crown. He seems the archetypal Prussian officer with duelling scars on his left cheek. His walking-out uniform has his NSDAP badge pinned to the left breast pocket and swastika brassard on the left sleeve. The SA Officers' belt in brown leather has a clasp buckle in a gilt-washed metal. Note that the dark straight-leg dress trousers have two strips of satin running down the outside seams.

This NSDAP officer of unknown rank wears a greatcoat over his tunic. The facings of the large collars are a lighter coffee-brown than the brown coat material and have piping around the upper collar piece. His Officers' belt is worn over and around the coat and he wears the swastika brassard on his left sleeve.

This Sturmabteilung (SA) Sturmann (stormtrooper/private) is wearing his brown tie and shirt, the collar of which displays his unit number on the right and his rank on his left and has twisted cord around the edges. His single shoulder strap (worn on the right shoulder) is also corded as per regulations for ORs. His brown leather belt has a pressed brass buckle and cross-strap. The swastika brassard is worn on the left arm and he wears an SA sports badge on his left breast pocket. His SA ORs' cap (kepi) has stiff sides and top with a cloth-covered peak. His breeches are tucked into high leather marching boots.

We have a good view of this SA Obersturmführer (1st lieutenant), with his bullion shoulder board and twisted cord collar patches. His four-pocket brown tunic replaced the simple brown shirt of earlier years, but the brown tie is retained. He has an SA sports badge on his pleated left breast pocket and the ubiquitous swastika brassard on his left arm.

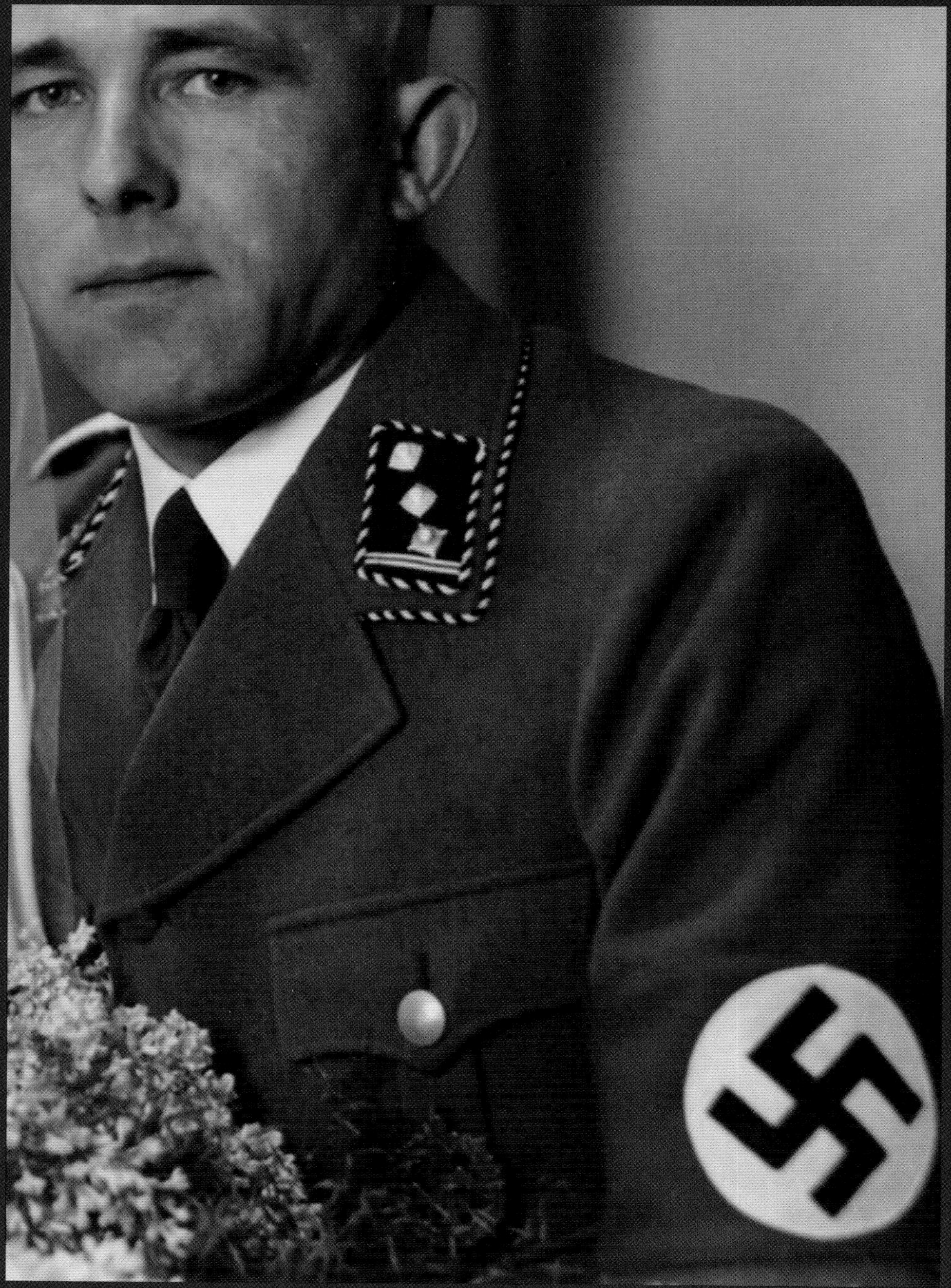

This SA man's rank collar patch could be a single Sturmann or a double Rottenführer stripe. Again we see the twisted cord collar and shoulder strap. His kepi carries the 1927 pattern political eagle. The false flaps of the cap have a 14mm silver-coloured button on the front and a leather chinstrap. He wears the brown shirt with pleated pockets and his brown tie carries the NSDAP enamel badge. He wears a religious floral sprig on his left breast and below that an NSDAP 1933 Nuremburg Party Day badge. The regulation belt with cross-strap can be seen more clearly here as well as the support hooks. He wears breeches and long leather marching boots. Just below his swastika brassard is his drivers' qualification badge of pressed metal on a black cloth diamond.

■ This SA Scharführer (squad leader/NCO) wears his post-1933 four-pocket tunic with a single pip rank patch. His belt is the Officers' pattern, very similar to the army type with a two-pronged buckle, but retaining the cross-strap. The NSDAP enamel badge appears on his brown tie and the swastika brassard on his left sleeve just above his drivers' qualification badge. His breeches are a dark colour, probably black and high marching boots are worn. The cloth-covered peak of his kepi is clearly shown, but just visible is his 1939 pattern SA cap eagle.

The Obertruppführer (senior troop leader) at the centre of this wedding-day photograph has the 1933 political cap eagle insignia on his kepi. His post-1927 SA Dienstrock (Service tunic) carries a floral sprig on his left lapel and his SA Treffen-Braunschweig 1931 (SA meeting commemorative award) and his SA sports badge. Under his right breast pocket is his whistle lanyard. On both cuffs we see his Alte Kampfer (old fighter) bullion stripes and in his gloved left hand is held an SA dress dagger. Straight trousers have replaced the riding breeches, and shoes, the marching boots. His right collar patch denotes his Standarte number, unfortunately unclear.

A rare photograph of a Marine SA-Scharführer. His tunic is Navy-Blue and his buttons and braiding are in gilt, note the anchor insignia on his right collar patch. His tunic is the same cut as the normal post 1933 SA Dienstrock and his belt and cross-strap is in black leather rather than brown. He too wears the swastika Brassard and his headwear is a vulkanfibre-visored service cap with gilt bullion cockade and gilt-washed pressed metal eagle rather than the cylindrical SA kepi.

A rather sombre-looking wedding group. This Truppführer leaves the registry offices preceded by two children, the boy in his Kriegsmarine outfit and the girl demonstrating her NSDAP zeal. The groom wears his SA Dienstrock with floral sprig and a swastika brassard. Just under the book that he carries (possibly a wedding copy of Mein Kampf) is his SA dress dagger. He has a whistle lanyard under his right breast pocket. The kepi carries the 1927 pattern political eagle in pressed metal.

This SA trooper has a blank rank collar patch signifying that he is an SA Mann (private). His Dienstrock (Service tunic) clearly shows the single corded shoulder strap and unit collar patch, which indicates his district. An enamel NSDAP badge, brassard and Officers'-style belt and cross-strap complete the picture.

This SA Sturmführer (2nd lieutenant) and bride are surrounded by family, friends and colleagues. Working across the group left to right, is an SA Gruppenführer (major-general), an army officer in Full Dress uniform, an army OR and behind him another SA Officer. At the rear, an air force NCO, possibly another SA officer, an elderly, highly decorated army Officer and at the back far right a naval Officer and two more SA Officers.

A high-ranking officer, this SA Brigadeführer (brigadier-general) is wearing his kepi with the broad silver bullion Tresse around the false flap, which reflects his rank. His rank collar patch of twin oak leaves and single pip is fairly clear while on the breast pocket of his Service tunic we see his World War I Iron Cross 1st Class. His Holbein-style SA dress dagger hangs from his Officers' belt and the breeches he wears are tucked into brown leather riding boots with spurs attached.

This beaming couple descend the steps at the top of which we see several SA Officers, one of them of high rank (from the rank stripes on his cuff). Our man, the groom, is wearing the white summer version of the SA Service tunic. His collar patch identifies him as having the rank of Sturmführer. On his left breast pocket are the DRL and SA sports badges and just to the left, his Hitler Jugend gold honour badge. His SA dress dagger is suspended from its hanger, through his tunic pocket. An SA lanyard hangs from his shoulder board.

This second photograph of the same newly-weds affords us a good view of the groom's headwear. It is the normal SA kepi with the 1939 SA eagle insignia in pressed metal above the single flap button. The leather sliding buckle chinstrap is also very clear in this shot. He has removed the wire crown stiffener from the cap giving it a more jaunty aspect. We can see clearly the twisted cord edging around his kepi, his collar patches and the bullion Officers' shoulder board.

In this rather formal wedding photograph, the bride wears a traditional black wedding dress and white veil. The groom wears an early SA brown shirt, breeches and high marching boots. He carries a small floral sprig on his left breast pocket and has the regulation ORs' belt and cross-strap. His kepi carries the 1927 pattern political eagle in pressed metal. His collar patches denote his unit on his right and on his left, his rank of Sturmann. His NSDAP enamel badge is pinned to his tie.

This SA junior officer displays the twisted cord shoulder board and collar edging. He has a whistle lanyard hanging from his right breast pocket and two 4mm silver bullion Tresse stripes on his cuff indicating length of service (one year).

This Zollbeamten (customs official) is wearing his 1938 parade uniform in grey-green with a dark green collar. His insignia and shoulder boards are of silver bullion and have RSV and a pip in pressed white metal. Around his left cuff is a flat machine-woven title of green with silver edging and a National Eagle insignia in the centre. He appears to have an enamel NSDAP badge on his left breast pocket. His rank is Zollwachtmeister (custom officer's assistant).

This groom is an officer of the Reichsforestdienst (state forestry service). His 1938 pattern Service Visor cap is grey-green cloth with a dark green headband. The piping around the crown and headband is also dark green. The Officers'-style cap cords are silver bullion and the 1937 political eagle insignia is in pressed metal and with a gold or silver wash, the wreath and cockade is embroidered silver bullion. His four-pocket tunic has a dark green upper collar with embroidered bullion rank patches. This particular man has the rank of Förster (lieutenant). He wears aiguillettes and has a religious floral sprig pinned to his tunic beside his medal and ribbon bar, which appear to be a mixture of World War I and World War II awards. His Officers' ivory-handled cutlass (short sword) hangs from the left side of his brocaded belt.

This Reichsbahn (state railways) station master wears his scarlet-topped Dienstmütze für Aufsichtsbeamte (Service cap) with its wire crown stiffener removed. It carries the 1936 pattern party eagle and its cockade is without any wreath cluster. His simple four-pocket Service tunic is unadorned except for his Reichbahn wheel and wing motif collar patches.

This Deutsche Luftsportverband or LDV (German air sports organisation) Rottenführer (corporal) is wearing his four-pocket blue-grey Service uniform with white shirt, black tie and yellow piping around the collar. He carries a floral sprig above his left breast pocket, below which is his Segelflieger (glider instructors' badge-grade B) and enamel NSDAP membership badge. His kepi-style cap is also blue-grey with yellow piping and has the later 1939 political eagle insignia in white pressed metal above the false flap button. The LDV became the Nationalsozialistisches Flieger Korps (NSFK) in 1935.

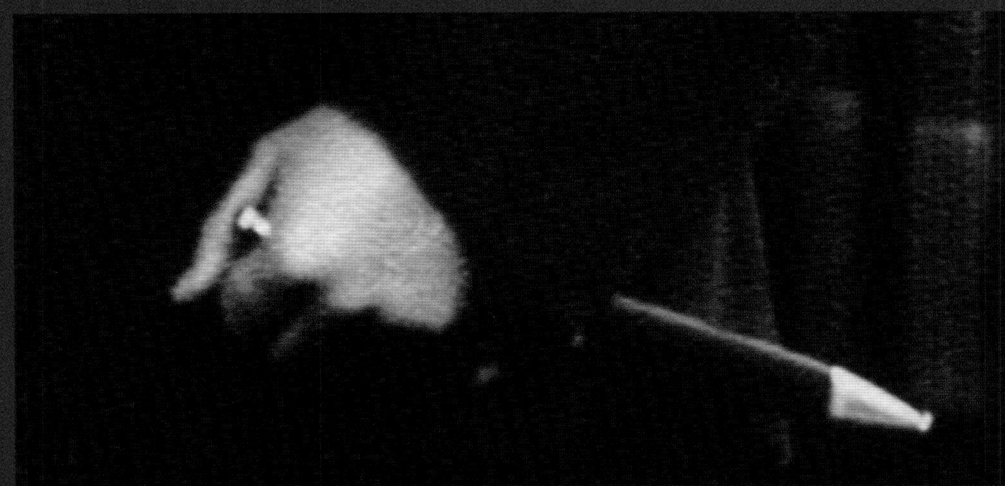

This more mature NSFK Rottenführer wears his Service uniform with his group number in pressed white metal on his right collar tab. The machine embroidered NSFK insignia of an Icarus-style figure was originally worn on the upper right arm but was moved to above the right breast pocket sometime after 1935. The ribbons on his left breast pocket appear to be the World War I Iron Cross 2nd Class and War Merit Cross 2nd Class with Swords and below that, his enamel NSDAP membership badge. He holds his second pattern LDV dress dagger in his left hand.

This groom is a member of the Reichsarbeitsdienstes or RAD (reich labour service). He wears the four-pocket Dress tunic which is in an earth-brown cloth with the upright collar in a darker chocolate brown. His collar patches are in silver bullion and red on a black backing. The machine-embroidered spade emblem on his left upper arm indicates his administrative county area and below that is his NSDAP brassard. On his cuff, dark green piping indicates administrative duties. An RAD service medal hangs from his left breast and he has an Officers' brocade belt and an RAD hewer (wide-bladed dagger) on his left thigh. His Filzmütze (felt, or so-called 'Robin Hood' cap) piped in silver for officers, is held in his right hand. This style of cap was replaced after 1943 by a variation of the Einheitsfeldmütze.

Another RAD man, this time a Truppführer (troop leader, NCO). His Service tunic has a turndown collar, the upper part being in the dark chocolate brown and the rest of the tunic in earth brown. He appears to have a large gold enamel NSDAP badge on his tie and on his left breast pocket he has his RAD service medal, Deutshcher Reichsbund fur Leibesubungen (DRL) and SA sports badges. The spade insignia above his NSDAP brassard suggests he is a group staff member and the black Armelstreifen (armstripe) around his left cuff indicates that he is working on the Siegfried Line, the gothic letter 'P' referring to the particular sector of the line. Other sectors were marked 'M', 'N', and 'O', but the wearing of these bands was discontinued after April 1941. His NCOs' hewer hangs from his left side and his felt Service cap has coloured piping with the RAD insignia in pressed white metal, of a spade between two stems of barley. On the side of his cap we can just see a pressed metal edelweiss badge.

This wedding photograph shows a Feldgendarme (military policeman) Unteroffizier from an unusual unit. He is a member of the Feldherrnhalle regiment (later a division), named after the detachment guarding the Feldherrnhalle monument in Munich. Members of that unit had to have served in the SA to qualify. His 1943 Field Service tunic carries his NCO Tresse around the upper collar and he has a Winter Campaign in the East medal ribbon in his buttonhole. Barely visible on his right breast is a whistle and lanyard. On his left cuff he wears the Feldherrnhalle title in SA brown material with flat machine-woven silver thread in Sütterlin script. Below that is his Feldgendarmerie cuff title.

The Authors

Brana Radovic has been a long-time collector of militaria, mainly steel helmets. He bought his first German helmet (model 42) at the age of eleven whilst on holiday with his family in the Channel Islands, the only part of the UK to have been occupied by Germany in World War II. He studied communication design and sculpture at art college. He began his career in the newspaper business, initially as an illustrator. He eventually found his way to the Financial Times in London where he worked for twenty-seven happy years as an illustrator and graphic designer, finally becoming its visual editor. On retirement, he and his wife Anna (and their cat) moved to south-west France where he does all the things a regular office job would not allow.

Frank Holford lives in South London with his wife June. He has two children, Richard and Catherine and five grandchildren. He continues to research and collect any pieces of interest from the period: "In 1974 I opened a tin box to rediscover the German pilots qualification badge which had been given to me by a friend of my father when he returned home from World War II. This was the start of my interest in all aspects of the World War II. I started to collect pieces that included the photographs of weddings that you see in this book. Brana and I met whilst working at the Financial Times and friendship started based on our shared interest in World War II. Over the years we took several road trips through Europe, with my son, to visit historically important sites of events in the war, meeting people who told us their stories and showed us 'bits' of their war."

THE HOMECOMING: the last prisoners of war, kept by the western allies, are returned to Germany. Berlin, August 1948